Microsoft®
Outlook 2000®
Brief Edition

INTERACTIVE COMPUTING SERIES

Kenneth C. Laudon
Michael W. Domis

Azimuth Interactive, Inc.

APPROVED COURSEWARE

Microsoft® OFFICE

APPROVED COURSEWARE

Irwin McGraw-Hill

Boston   Burr Ridge, IL   Dubuque, IA   Madison, WI   New York   San Francisco   St. Louis
Bangkok   Bogotá   Caracas   Lisbon   London   Madrid   Mexico City   Milan   New Delhi   Seoul
Singapore   Sydney   Taipei   Toronto

McGraw-Hill Higher Education

*A Division of The **McGraw-Hill** Companies*

MICROSOFT OUTLOOK 2000 BRIEF EDITION

1 2 3 4 5 6 7 8 9 0 QPD/QPD 9 0 9 8 7 6 5 4 3 2 1 0 9

ISBN 0-07-235858-0

Vice president/Editor-in-Chief: *Michael W. Junior*
Publisher: *David Kendric Brake*
Sponsoring editor: *Trisha O'Shea*
Associate editor: *Steve Schuetz*
Developmental editor: *Erin Riley*
Senior marketing manager: *Jeff Parr*
Project manager: *Pat Frederickson*
Production supervisor: *Michael R. McCormick*
Freelance design coordinator: *Pam Verros*
Cover illustration: *Kip Henrie*
Supplement coordinator: *Matthew Perry*
New Media: *Lisa Ramos-Torrescan*
Compositor: *Azimuth Interactive, Inc.*
Typeface: *10/12 Sabon*
Printer: *Quebecor Printing Book Group/Dubuque*

Library of Congress Catalog Card Number: 99-069671

www.mhhe.com

Microsoft® Outlook 2000® Brief Edition

INTERACTIVE COMPUTING SERIES

Kenneth C. Laudon
Michael W. Domis

Azimuth Interactive, Inc.

APPROVED COURSEWARE

At **McGraw-Hill Higher Education**, we publish instructional materials targeted at the higher education market. In an effort to expand the tools of higher learning, we publish texts, lab manuals, study guides, testing materials, software, and multimedia products.

At **Irwin/McGraw-Hill** (a division of McGraw-Hill Higher Education), we realize technology will continue to create new mediums for professors and students to manage resources and communicate information with one another. We strive to provide the most flexible and complete teaching and learning tools available and offer solutions to the changing world of teaching and learning.

Irwin/McGraw-Hill is dedicated to providing the tools necessary for today's instructors and students to navigate the world of Information Technology successfully.

Seminar Series - Irwin/McGraw-Hill's Technology Connection seminar series offered across the country every year, demonstrates the latest technology products and encourages collaboration among teaching professionals.

Osborne/McGraw-Hill - A division of the McGraw-Hill Companies known for its best-selling Internet titles *Harley Hahn's Internet & Web Yellow Pages* and the *Internet Complete Reference*, offers an additional resource for certification and has strategic publishing relationships with corporations such as Corel Corporation and America Online. For more information, visit Osborne at www.osborne.com.

Digital Solutions - Irwin/McGraw-Hill is committed to publishing Digital Solutions. Taking your course online doesn't have to be a solitary venture. Nor does it have to be a difficult one. We offer several solutions, which will let you enjoy all the benefits of having course material online. For more information, visit www.mhhe.com/solutions/index.mhtml.

Packaging Options - For more about our discount options, contact your local Irwin/McGraw-Hill Sales representative at 1-800-338-3987, or visit our Web site at www.mhhe.com/it.

Irwin McGraw-Hill

Preface

Interactive Computing Series

Goals/Philosophy

The *Interactive Computing Series* provides you with an illustrated interactive environment for learning software skills using Microsoft Office. The Interactive Computing Series is composed of both text and multimedia interactive CD-ROMs. The text and the CD-ROMs are closely coordinated. *It's up to you. You can choose how you want to learn.*

Approach

The *Interactive Computing Series* is the visual interactive way to develop and apply software skills. This skills-based approach coupled with its highly visual, two-page spread design allows the student to focus on a single skill without having to turn the page. A running case study is provided through the text, reinforcing the skills and giving a real-world focus to the learning process.

Approved Microsoft Courseware

Use of the Microsoft User Specialist Approved Courseware Logo on this product signifies that it has been independently reviewed and approved in complying with the following standards: Acceptable coverage of all content related to the Microsoft Office Exam entitled *Microsoft Outlook 2000* and sufficient performance-based exercises that relate closely to all required content, based on sampling of text. For further information on Microsoft's MOUS certification program please visit Microsoft's Web site at www.mous.net.

APPROVED COURSEWARE

About the Book

The Interactive Computing Series offers *two levels* of instruction.
Each level builds upon the previous level.

Brief lab manual - covers the basics of the application, contains four chapters.
Introductory lab manual - includes the material in the Brief textbook plus four additional chapters. The Introductory lab manuals prepare students for the *Microsoft Office User Specialist Proficiency Exam (MOUS Certification)*.

Each lesson is organized around **Skills**, **Concepts**, and **Steps (Do It!)**.

> Each lesson is divided into a number of Skills. Each **Skill** is first explained at the top of the page.
> Each **Concept** is a concise description of why the skill is useful and where it is commonly used.
> Each **Step (Do It!)** contains the instructions on how to complete the skill.

About the CD-ROM

The CD-ROM provides a unique interactive environment for students where they learn to use software faster and remember it better. The CD-ROM is organized similar to the books: The **Skill** is defined, the **Concept** is explained in rich multimedia, and the student performs **Steps (Do It!)** within sections called Interactivities. There are at least 45 Interactivities per CD-ROM. Some of the features of the CD-ROM are:

Simulated Environment - The Interactive Computing CD-ROM places students in a simulated controlled environment where they can practice and perform the skills of the application software.
Interactive Exercises - The student is asked to demonstrate command of a specific software skill. The student's actions are followed by a digital "TeacherWizard" that provides feedback.
SmartQuizzes - Provide performance-based assessment of the student at the end of each lesson.

Using the Book

In the book, each skill is described in a two-page graphical spread (Figure 1). The left side of the two-page spread describes the skill, the concept, and the steps needed to perform the skill. The right side of the spread uses screen shots to show you how the screen should look at key stages.

Figure 1

Skill: Each lesson is divided into a number of specific skills

Concept: A concise description of why the skill is useful and where it is commonly used

Running case: A real-world case ties the skill and the concept to a practical situation

Do It!: Step-by-step directions show you how to use the skill

Skill

Using the Recycle Bin

Concept

The Recycle Bin is a storage place for files that have been deleted. Files that you no longer need should be deleted in order to save disk space and maximize the efficiency of your computer. If you decide that you need a file again, or have accidentally deleted a file, you can rescue it from the Recycle Bin. If you know you will never need a file again, you can delete the file permanently.

Do It!

Delete the Copy of Alice and To Be Deleted folders from your hard drive. Then rescue To Be Deleted from the Recycle Bin. Finally, delete the shortcut from your hard drive permanently.

1. Click the Start button, highlight Programs, then select Windows Explorer.

2. Click the plus next to the My Student Files folder to expand it. The two folders nested in the My Student Files folder will appear in the hierarchy.

3. Select the Copy of Alice folder, then click the Delete button on the Standard Buttons toolbar. The Confirm Folder Delete dialog box (Figure 2-20) will appear, asking you if are sure you want to move the folder to the Recycle Bin.

4. Click [Yes]. The dialog box will close and the folder will be moved to the Recycle Bin.

5. Click the Close button to exit Windows Explorer.

6. Click and drag the To Be Deleted folder from the desktop to the Recycle Bin. When the Recycle Bin becomes highlighted, release the mouse button. The Confirm Folder Delete dialog box will appear.

7. Click Yes to delete the folder.

8. Double-click the Recycle Bin. The Recyle Bin window will open. Figure 2-21 shows the inside of the Recycle Bin displaying all the files and folder you have sent there.

9. Drag the To Be Deleted folder from the Recycle Bin window to an empty space on the desktop. The folder appears on the desktop, and is now an accessible item that can be used. Items still in the Recycle Bin cannot be opened.

10. Right-click the To Be Deleted folder and choose the Delete command from the pop-up menu to send the folder back into the Recycle Bin.

11. Click File, then select Empty Recyle Bin. The Confirm Multiple File Delete dialog box will appear.

12. Click Yes to permanently delete the folders from your hard drive.

13. Click the Close button to shut the Recycle Bin window.

44

End-of-Lesson Features

In the book, the learning in each lesson is reinforced at the end by a quiz and a skills review called Interactivity, which provides step-by-step exercises and real-world problems for the students to solve independently.

Windows 98

More

Summary tables: Tables give you a quick overview of shortcuts and toolbar icons needed to use the skills

Table 2-1 Ways to delete or restore a selected file

TO DELETE	TO RESTORE
Click the Delete button on the toolbar	Click the Undo button on the toolbar
Right-click and select Delete from the pop-up menu	Right-click the file in the Recycle Bin and select Restore
Drag the file to the Recycle Bin	Drag the file from the Recycle Bin to any location
Press [Delete]	Go to the File menu in the Recycle Bin and select Restore

Figure 2-20 Confirm Folder Delete dialog box

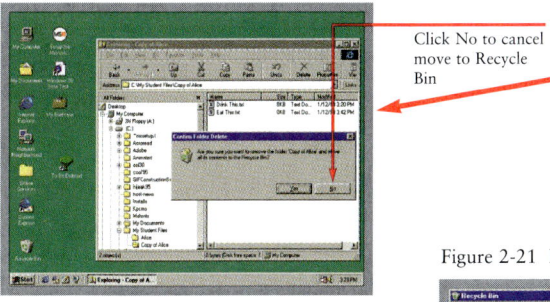

Click No to cancel move to Recycle Bin

Screen shots: Screen shots show you what the screen should like after following the Do It! steps

Figure 2-21 Recycle Bin window

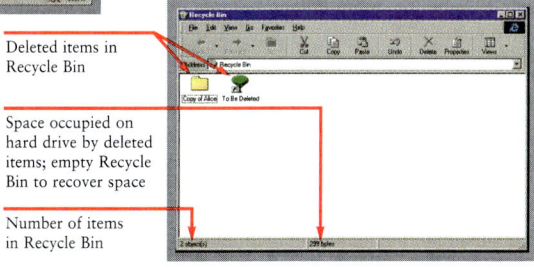

Deleted items in Recycle Bin

Space occupied on hard drive by deleted items; empty Recycle Bin to recover space

Number of items in Recycle Bin

Practice

Move the shortcut you created in the last skill to the Recycle Bin. Then move the shortcut out of the Recycle Bin and back to the desktop. Delete the shortcut a second time using a different technique. This time, delete the shortcut permanently.

Hot Tip

Files can be erased immediately without being stored in the Recycle Bin. Right-click the Recycle Bin, then select Properties. On the View tab, uncheck the "Display delete confimation dialog box" command. This enables you to delete files in one step.

45

Hot Tip: Gives you advice on how to use the software and warns you of potential problems

Practice: Allows you to practice the skill with a built-in exercise or directs you to a student file

Using the Interactive CD-ROM

The Interactive Computing multimedia CD-ROM provides an unparalleled learning environment in which you can learn software skills faster and better than in books alone. The CD-ROM creates a unique interactive environment in which you can learn to use software faster and remember it better. The CD-ROM uses the same lessons, skills, concepts, and Do It! steps as found in the book, but presents the material using voice, video, animation, and precise simulation of the software you are learning. A typical CD-ROM contents screen shows the major elements of a lesson (see Figure 2 below).

Skills list: A list of skills allows you to jump directly to any skill you want to learn or review, including interactive sessions with the TeacherWizard

Figure 2

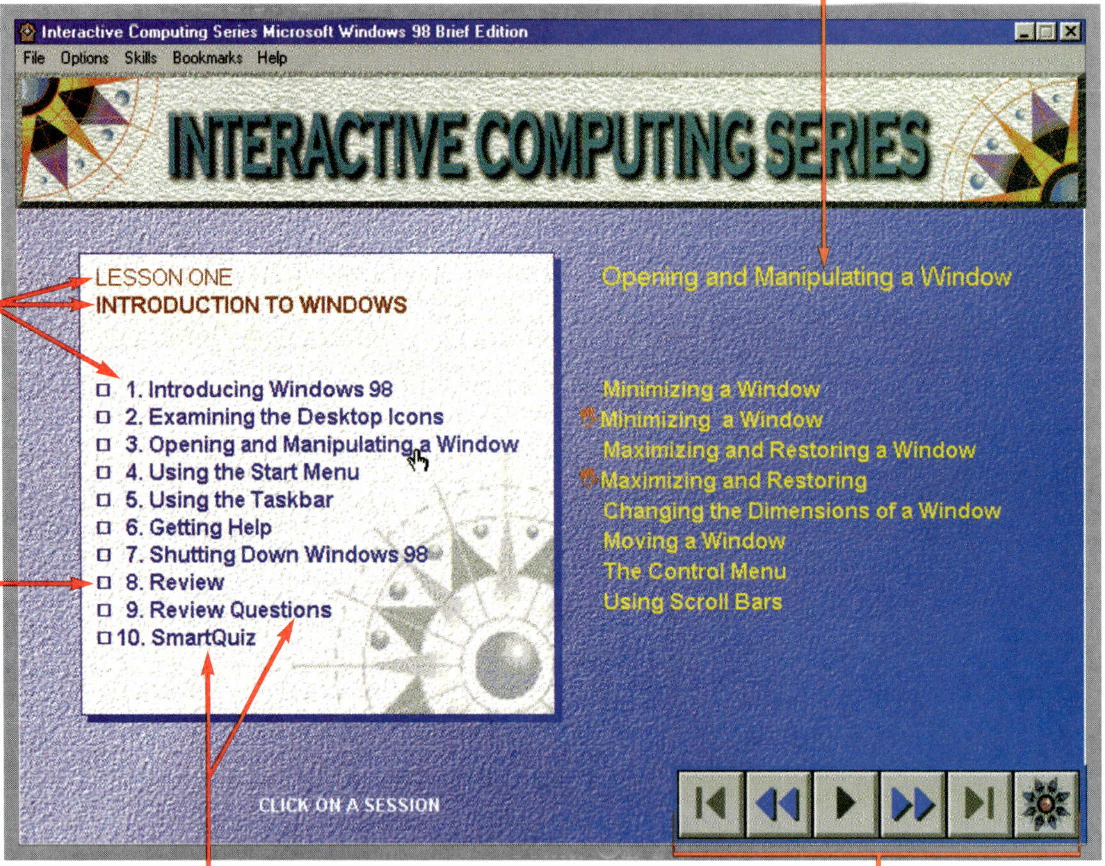

Interactive Computing Series Microsoft Windows 98 Brief Edition

File   Options   Skills   Bookmarks   Help

INTERACTIVE COMPUTING SERIES

Lessons and skills: The lessons and skills covered in the CD are coordinated closely with those in the book

LESSON ONE
INTRODUCTION TO WINDOWS

☐ 1. Introducing Windows 98
☐ 2. Examining the Desktop Icons
☐ 3. Opening and Manipulating a Window
☐ 4. Using the Start Menu
☐ 5. Using the Taskbar
☐ 6. Getting Help
☐ 7. Shutting Down Windows 98
☐ 8. Review
☐ 9. Review Questions
☐ 10. SmartQuiz

Opening and Manipulating a Window

Minimizing a Window
Minimizing a Window
Maximizing and Restoring a Window
Maximizing and Restoring
Changing the Dimensions of a Window
Moving a Window
The Control Menu
Using Scroll Bars

CLICK ON A SESSION

Review: The review summarizes the skills you have learned in a lesson and allows you to return to a skill by clicking its title

Review Questions and SmartQuiz: Review Questions test your knowledge of the concepts covered in the lesson; SmartQuiz tests your ability to accomplish tasks in a simulated software environment

User controls: Precise and simple user controls permit you to start, stop, pause, jump forward or backward one sentence, or jump forward or backward an entire skill. A single navigation star takes you back to the lesson's table of contents

Unique Features of the CD-ROM: TeacherWizard™ and SmartQuiz™

Interactive Computing: Software Skills offers many leading-edge features on the CD-ROM currently found in no other learning product on the market. One such feature is *interactive exercises* in which you are asked to demonstrate your command of a software skill in a precisely simulated software environment. Your actions are followed closely by a digital TeacherWizard that guides you with additional information if you make a mistake. When you complete the action called for by the TeacherWizard correctly, you are congratulated and prompted to continue the lesson. If you make a mistake, the TeacherWizard gently lets you know: "No, that's not the right icon. Click on the Folder icon on the left side of the top toolbar to open a file." No matter how many mistakes you make, the TeacherWizard is there to help you.

Another leading-edge feature is the end-of-lesson SmartQuiz. Unlike the multiple choice and matching questions found in the book quiz, the SmartQuiz puts you in a simulated digital software world and asks you to show your mastery of skills while actually working with the software (Figure 3).

Figure 3

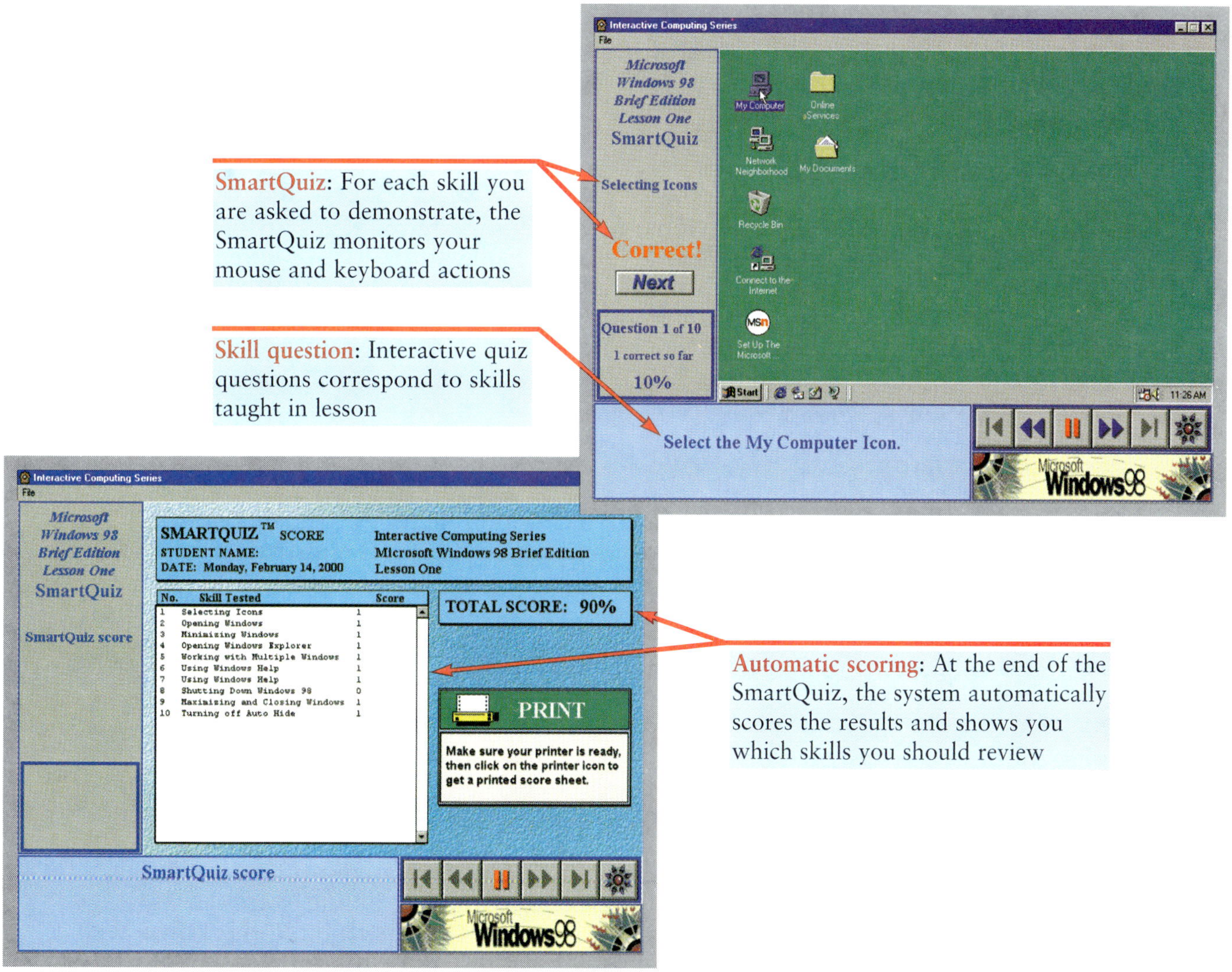

SmartQuiz: For each skill you are asked to demonstrate, the SmartQuiz monitors your mouse and keyboard actions

Skill question: Interactive quiz questions correspond to skills taught in lesson

Automatic scoring: At the end of the SmartQuiz, the system automatically scores the results and shows you which skills you should review

Teaching Resources

The following is a list of supplemental material available with the Interactive Computing Series:

SimNet (Simulated Network Assessment Product) - Tests student software skills in a safe, simulated environment. SimNet performance-based questions are mapped to MOUS certification skills. Complete student tracking and skill-by-skill reporting system is included. SimNet is available in CD-Rom, and in network and Web versions.

ATLAS Active Testing and Learning Assessment Software - available for the Interactive Computing Series, is our cutting edge "Real TimeAssessment" software. ATLAS is web-enabled and allows students to perform timed tasks while working live in an application. ATLAS will track how a specific task is completed and the time it takes to complete that task. ATLAS measures Proficiency and Efficiency ("It's not only what you do but how you do it."). ATLAS will provide full customization and authoring capabilities for professors, and includes content from all of our application Series.

Instructor's Resource Kits

The Instructor's Resource Kit provides professors with all of the ancillary material needed to teach a course. Irwin/McGraw-Hill is dedicated to providing instructors with the most effective instruction resources available. Many of these resources are available at our Information Technology Supersite www.mhhe.com/it. Our Instructor's Kits are available on CD-ROM and contain the following:

> **Diploma by Brownstone** - is the most flexible, powerful, and easy-to-use computerized testing system available in higher education. The diploma system allows professors to create an Exam as a printed version, as a LAN-based Online version, and as an Internet version. Diploma includes grade book features, which automate the entire testing process.
> **Instructor's Manual** - Includes:
> -Solutions to all lessons and end-of-unit material
> -Teaching Tips
> -Teaching Strategies
> -Additional exercises
> **Student Data Files** - To use the Interactive Computing Series, students must have Student Data Files to complete practice and test sessions. The instructor and students using this text in classes are granted the right to post the student files on any network or stand-alone computer, or to distribute the files on individual diskettes. The student files may be downloaded from our IT Supersite at www.mhhe.com/it.
> **Series Web Site** - Available at www.mhhe.com/cit/apps/laudon.

Digital Solutions

> **Pageout Lite** - is designed if you're just beginning to explore Web site options. Pageout Lite is great for posting your own material online. You may choose one of three templates, type in your material, and Pageout Lite instantly converts it to HTML.
> **Pageout** - is our Course Web site Development Center. Pageout offers a Syllabus page, Web site address, Online Learning Center Content, online exercises and quizzes, gradebook, discussion board, an area for students to build their own Web pages, and all the features of Pageout Lite. For more information please visit the Pageout Web site at www.mhla.net/pageout.

Teaching Resources (continued)

OLC/Series Web Sites - Online Learning Centers (OLCs)/Series Sites are accessible through our Supersite at www.mhhe.com/it. Our Online Learning Centers/Series Sites provide pedagogical features and supplements for our titles online. Students can point and click their way to key terms, learning objectives, chapter overviews, PowerPoint slides, exercises, and Web links.

The McGraw-Hill Learning Architecture (MHLA) - is a complete course delivery system. MHLA gives professors ownership in the way digital content is presented to the class through online quizzing, student collaboration, course administration, and content management. For a walk-through of MHLA visit the MHLA Web site at www.mhla.net.

Packaging Options - For more about our discount options, contact your local Irwin/McGraw-Hill Sales representative at 1-800-338-3987 or visit our Web site at www.mhhe.com/it.

Visit www.mhhe.com/it
THE ONLY SITE WITH ALL YOUR CIT AND MIS NEEDS.

Acknowledgments

The Interactive Computing Series is a cooperative effort of many individuals, each contributing to an overall team effort. The Interactive Computing team is composed of instructional designers, writers, multimedia designers, graphic artists, and programmers. Our goal is to provide you and your instructor with the most powerful and enjoyable learning environment using both traditional text and new interactive multimedia techniques. Interactive Computing is tested rigorously in both CD-ROM and text formats prior to publication.

Our special thanks to Trisha O'Shea, our Editor for computer applications and concepts. And to Jodi McPherson, Marketing Director for Computer Information Systems. Both Trisha and Jodi have provided exceptional market awareness and understanding, along with enthusiasm and support for the project. They have inspired us all to work closely together. Steven Schuetz provided valuable technical review of our interactive versions, and Charles Pelto provided superb quality assurance. Thanks to our new Publisher David Brake, and Mike Junior, Vice President and Editor-in-Chief. They have given us tremendous encouragement and the needed support to tackle seemingly impossible projects.

The Azimuth team members who contributed to the textbooks and CD-ROM multimedia program are:

Ken Rosenblatt (Textbooks Project Manager and Writer)
Russell Polo (Chief Programmer)
Steven D. Pileggi (Multimedia Project Director)
Jason Eiseman (Technical Writer)
Michael W. Domis (Technical Writer)
Robin Pickering (Developmental Editor, Quality Assurance)
Stefon Westry (Multimedia Designer)
Caroline Kasterine (Multimedia Designer, Writer)
Joseph S. Gina (Multimedia Designer)
Irene Pileggi (Multimedia Designer)
Josie Torlish (Quality Assurance)

Contents

Outlook 2000 Brief Edition

Contents

Continued

Foreword

Setting Up Your Internet Connection

When you first install Outlook 2000 on your computer, you will be asked to choose one of the three E-mail Service Options: No E-mail; Internet Only or Corporate/Workgroup. If you are planning to use Outlook to organize your tasks, meetings and events, but wish to use another program to send and receive e-mail, you should choose the No E-mail option. If you do wish to use Outlook to send and receive e-mail, you must choose one of the two other options: Internet Only or Corporate/Workgroup. If you are installing Outlook 2000 on a computer that is not part of a network, you should choose the Internet Only option. If your computer is part of a network, the Corporate/Workgroup option may be more appropriate.

To send and receive e-mail using Outlook 2000, you will also need to set up an Internet e-mail account through an Internet Service Provider (ISP) that uses the POP3/STMP or IMAP4 protocols. America Online, for example, does not use these protocols. You will need to check with your ISP to find out the names and port numbers designated for your incoming (POP3 or IMAP4) and outgoing (STMP) mail servers, and whether your outgoing mail server requires authentication. You will also need your e-mail address, account or logon name, and password. You should set up your Outlook Internet E-mail account when you first install Outlook 2000, by following the Startup wizard's instructions.

Select no email

L E S S O N

1

INTRODUCING OUTLOOK 2000

Microsoft Outlook is an integrated task, scheduling and communications management program. Learning to use it will improve your ability to organize your time and stay abreast of your correspondence in a business or personal environment. With Outlook, you can do away with physical objects such as calendars, appointment books, task lists, and address books. Outlook stores all these items for you in one program where you can access them quickly and easily.

E-mail is rapidly becoming the preferred choice of correspondence in the business world combining the instantaneous communication of a phone call with written substantiation. Outlook 2000 provides you with an e-mail system integrated with your day-planner, calendar, and contacts.

In this book you will learn how to use Microsoft Outlook to open, reply to, send, and forward e-mail. You will work with attachments to e-mail and learn how to enhance the appearance of your mail with templates. You will then learn how to manage a calendar by scheduling appointments, events and meetings. Further, you will become familiar with the electronic Address Book, which will allow you to maintain information about your business contacts in one, easy to access location. You will learn how to create a Task list and how to use electronic notes. Finally, you will learn how to integrate several of Outlook's components into one functioning unit.

Case Study:
Virginia Reynolds is the Production Coordinator for a small publishing firm. Her job is to keep track of all the tasks pertinent to publishing each book, contact all those associated with the book, and schedule appointments for meetings when necessary. To aid her in her job, her employer has given her a copy of Outlook 2000. Virginia will begin by familiarizing herself with the application. Then, she will customize the program to suit her office enviroment.

Skill

Starting Outlook 2000

Concept

To use the Outlook 2000 program, or application, you must first open it. The act of opening an application is also called running, starting or launching. In the Windows environment, you can launch a program in a number of ways, including using desktop and Start menu shortcuts, using the Run command, double-clicking executable file icons, and clicking a Windows 98 Quick Launch toolbar button.

Do It!

Virginia wants to open the Outlook 2000 application so she can customize it to her work environment.

1. Make sure the computer, monitor, and any other necessary peripheral devices are turned on. The Windows desktop should appear on your screen.

2. Locate the Windows taskbar, usually at the bottom of the screen. Use the mouse to guide the pointer over the Start button **Start** , on the left side of the taskbar, and click the left mouse button. This action opens the Windows Start menu.

3. Move the mouse pointer up the Start menu to Programs, highlighting it. The Programs menu will be displayed as shown in **Figure 1-1**.

4. Position the pointer over **Microsoft Outlook** , highlighting it, and click once to open the application. (If Outlook is not there, try looking under Microsoft Office on the Start menu.) Outlook will open with the Outlook Today window displayed, as shown in **Figure 1-2**.

More

Each computer can vary in its setup depending on its hardware and software configurations. Therefore, your Outlook startup procedure may be slightly different from that described above. The Windows environment, from Windows 95 on, allows you to place shortcuts to a program's executable (.exe) file in various places. For example, the Outlook listing on the Program menu is a shortcut. You can also place shortcuts on the desktop, or even on the first level of the Start menu.

Because you can customize the Outlook program, your screen may not look exactly like the one shown to the right. As noted in the Foreword, there are three different ways to configure Outlook 2000: No E-mail, Internet Only, and Corporate/Workgroup. The functionality, and appearance of Outlook 2000 will differ depending on the option you choose. Unless otherwise indicated, the figures in this book show Outlook 2000 as it appears when the Corporate/Workgroup E-Mail Service option has been selected.

Figure 1-1 Using the Start menu

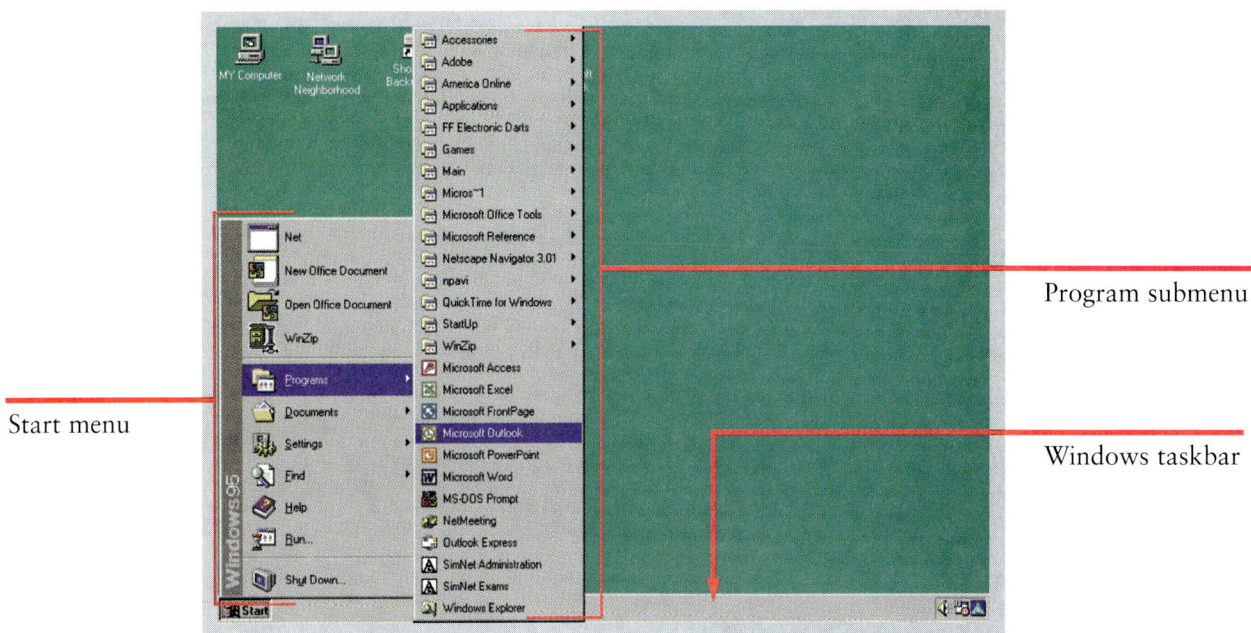

Start menu

Program submenu

Windows taskbar

Figure 1-2 Outlook Today window

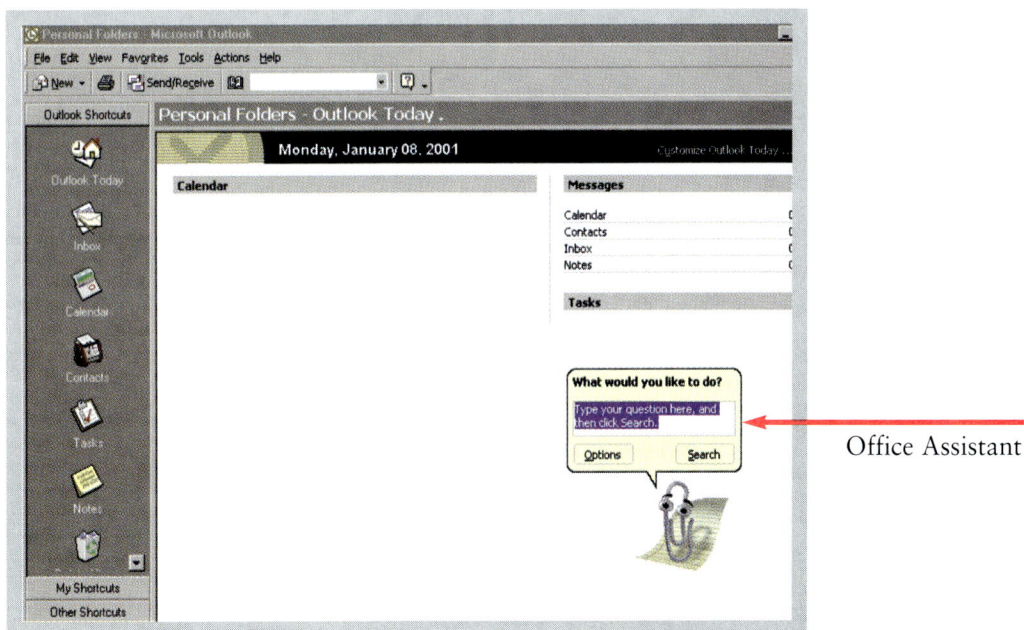

Office Assistant

Hot Tip

The **Office Assistant** shown in **Figure 1-2** is part of the Outlook Help facility and will be discussed in detail later in this lesson.

Skill Customizing Outlook Today

Concept

Outlook 2000 allows you to customize the Outlook Today window. You can choose to have those items on your Outlook Today screen that you use most frequently. Customizing Outlook Today will help maximize your efficiency as you use the program.

Do It!

Virginia will customize her Outlook Today screen.

1. If the Outlook Today folder is not currently active, activate it by clicking on its shortcut icon 🗂 in the Outlook Bar on the left side of the screen as in **Figure 1-3**.

2. Click on the words Customize Outlook Today in the upper-right corner of the Outlook Today screen.

3. In the Startup section, click the check box for When starting, go directly to Outlook Today.

4. In the Messages section, click the Choose Folders button. The `Choose Folders...` dialog box will open (**Figure 1-4**).

5. If they are not already checked, click the check boxes for the following folders: Calendar, Contacts, Inbox, and Notes. Click the OK button `OK`.

6. In the Tasks section, click the All Tasks radio button.

7. Click the arrow in the Styles section and select Standard (two column).

8. Click the Save Changes button. Your Outlook Today screen should now look like **Figure 1-5**.

More

The Outlook Today screen allows you to see several items at a glance. The Calendar portion will always display the current day's items. The Message section of the screen will keep you informed of any new messages in the folders you have selected and the Tasks section will keep you abreast of items that must be completed.

The section of the Outlook window that shows the Outlook Today information is called the Outlook Today Information viewer (see **Figure 1-5**). Each Outlook folder has its own Information viewer appropriate for the type of items in the folder. It is in the Information viewer that the major functions of Outlook are performed.

Figure 1-3 Outlook Bar

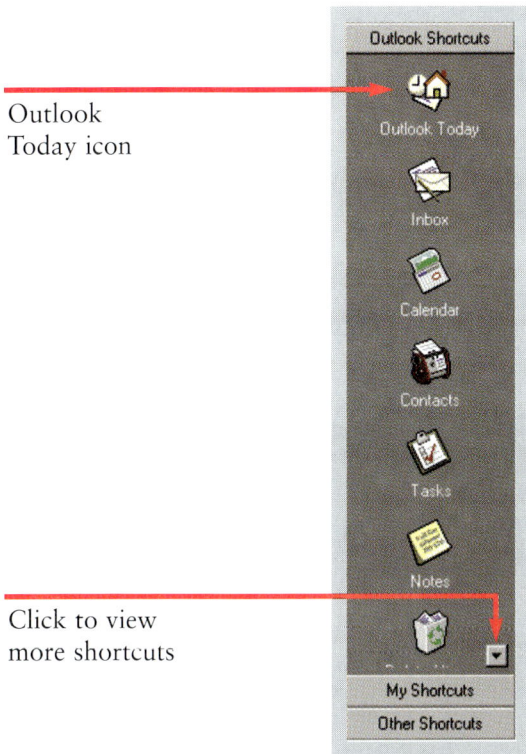

Outlook
Today icon

Click to view
more shortcuts

Figure 1-4 Choose Folders dialog box

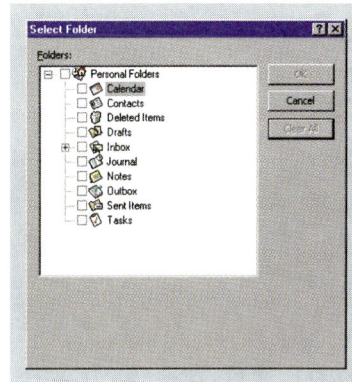

Figure 1-5 Customized Outlook Today window

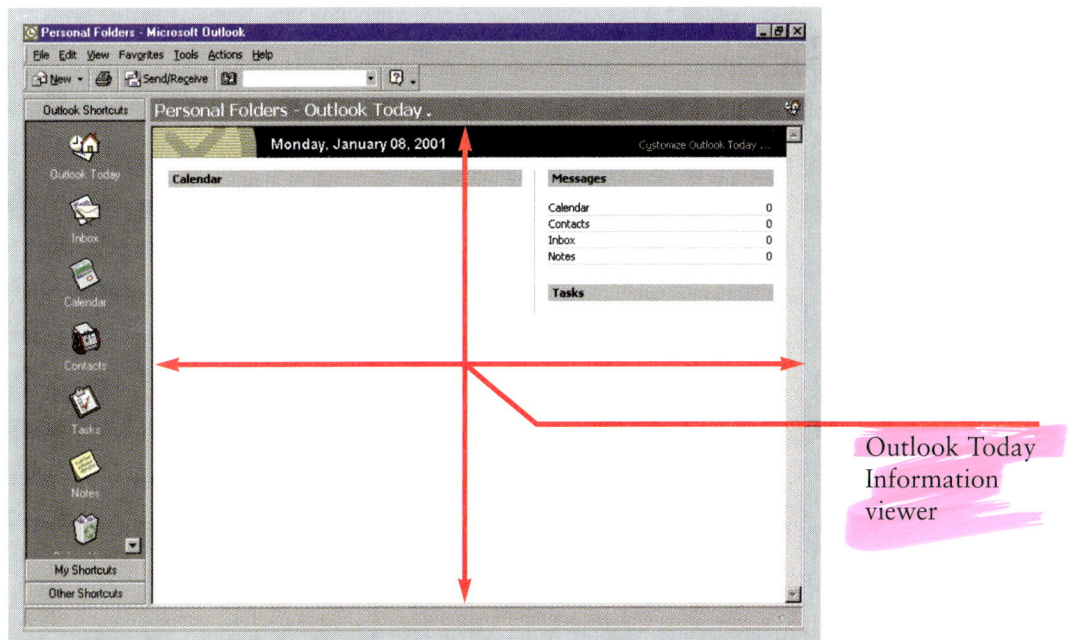

Outlook Today
Information
viewer

Practice

Customize the Outlook Today screen by changing it to **Summer** style, and then to **Winter** style. Finally, change it back to the **Standard (two column)** style.

Hot Tip

Every calendar entry, task and folder listed in the Outlook Today Information viewer is a hyperlink. You can use these links to quickly navigate within the Outlook program.

Navigating Between Components

Skill

Concept

Outlook provides a navigation bar to enable you to move quickly between components of the program and to other components of Office 2000 and the Windows operating system. This bar is called the Outlook Bar. Learning to use it will increase your efficiency in Outlook.

Do It!

Virginia will explore the Outlook Bar.

1 On the Outlook Bar (**Figure 1-6**), which is located on the left side of the Outlook screen and contains shortcut icons for Outlook Today, Inbox, Calendar, Contacts, Tasks, Notes and Deleted Items, click on Calendar 🗓.

2 To navigate quickly to Drafts, Outbox, Sent Items, Journal or Outlook Update (**Figure 1-7**), click on My Shortcuts My Shortcuts at the bottom of the Outlook Bar.

3 Click on Other Shortcuts in the Outlook Bar. Here, you will see shortcuts for My Computer, My Documents, and Favorites (**Figure 1-8**).

4 To get back to the original Outlook Bar view, click on Outlook Shortcuts which is now at the top of the Outlook Bar.

More

Another way to move to a different Outlook folder is to select it from the Folder List. Click the name of the current folder at the top of the Information viewer. For example, click Personal Folders-Outlook Today. The Folder List will open. Click the folder you want to switch to from the list. Click the pushpin 🖈 to keep the Folder List open.

Figure 1-6 Outlook Shortcuts

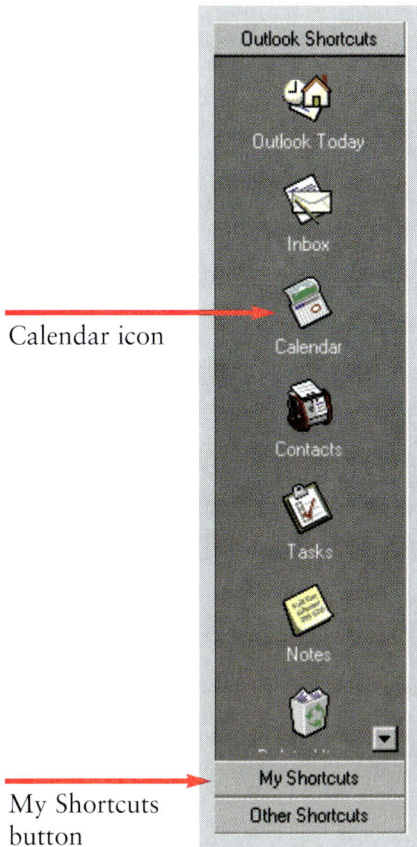

Figure 1-7 My Shortcuts

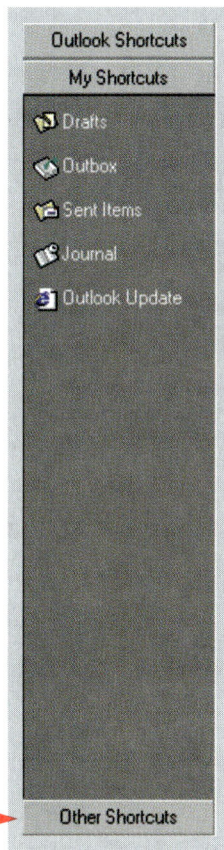

Figure 1-8 Other Shortcuts

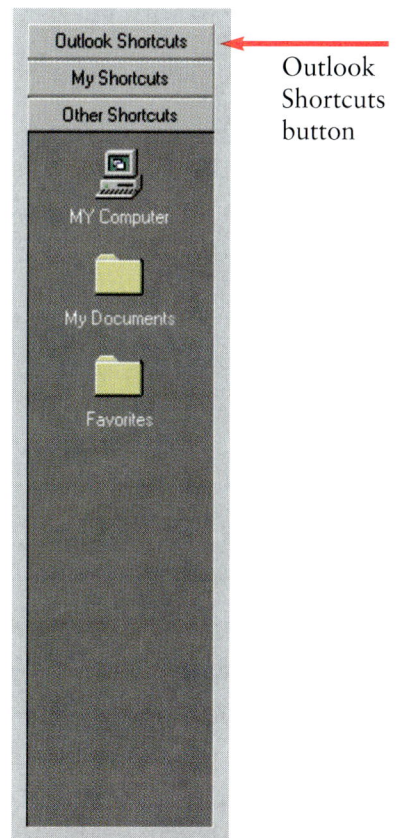

Calendar icon

My Shortcuts
button

Other Shortcuts button

Outlook
Shortcuts
button

Practice

Using the Outlook Bar, and the Outlook Today Information viewer, practice navigating between components of the program. Click on **Inbox**, **Tasks**, **Calendar**, **Notes**, then **Contacts**, and finally, return to **Outlook Today**.

Hot Tip

Any time you move the cursor arrow over an item and it turns into a pointing hand, you've found a shortcut.

Skill Using the Office Assistant

Concept

Even the most experienced users need help from time to time. The Office Assistant is a help facility that lets you ask a question relating to your problem. It will reply with several help options that may be useful to you based on the question you ask.

Do It!

Virginia has a question about Outlook 2000. She will use the Office Assistant to find out about some of Outlook's functions.

1. If the Office Assistant is not active, click 🔲 on the Standard toolbar. Otherwise, click the Office Assistant. A dialog balloon appears with the statement, Type your question here, and then click search highlighted.

2. In the text box, type What does the Office Assistant do? and then click Search. A list of topics appears in the balloon as shown in **Figure 1-9**.

3. Click the first topic, Display tips and messages through the Office Assistant. **Figure 1-10** shows the Microsoft Outlook Help window that appears.

4. Click on the Help topic Show the Tip of the Day when Outlook starts and read it.

5. When you've finished reading about the Tip of the Day, click the Close button ✖ in the upper-right corner of the Help screen.

6. Right-click the Office Assistant. Click the Hide command from the menu that appears to hide the Office Assistant.

More

From time to time the Assistant will offer tips on how to use Outlook more efficiently. The appearance of a small light bulb next to the Assistant indicates that there is a tip to be viewed. To view the tip, click the light bulb.

Furthermore, the Office Assistant can be customized. Click the Options button in the Office Assistant dialog balloon to open the Office Assistant dialog box. This dialog box has two tabs: Gallery and Options. The Gallery tab contains eight Assistants to choose from, and scrolling through the characters provides a preview of each one. The Options tab, shown in **Figure 1-11**, allows you to alter the Assistant's capabilities and decide what kinds of tips it will show.

Figure 1-10 Outlook Help window

Click here

Figure 1-9 Office Assistant dialog balloon

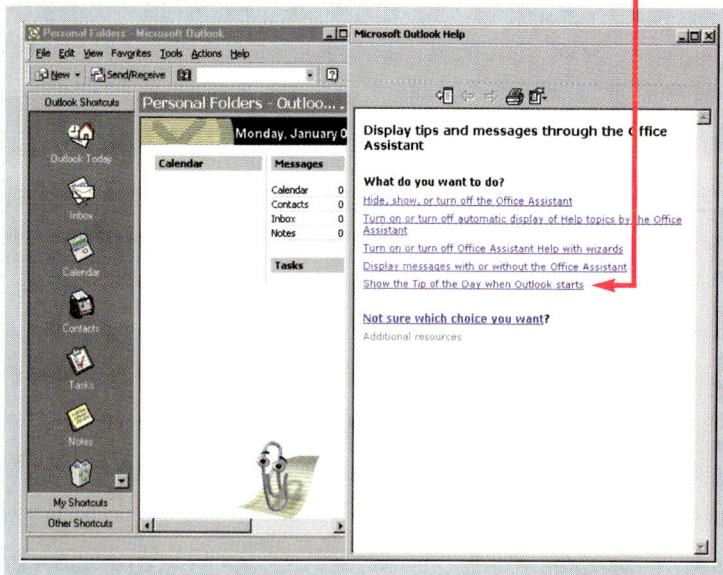

Figure 1-11 Office Assistant's Options tab

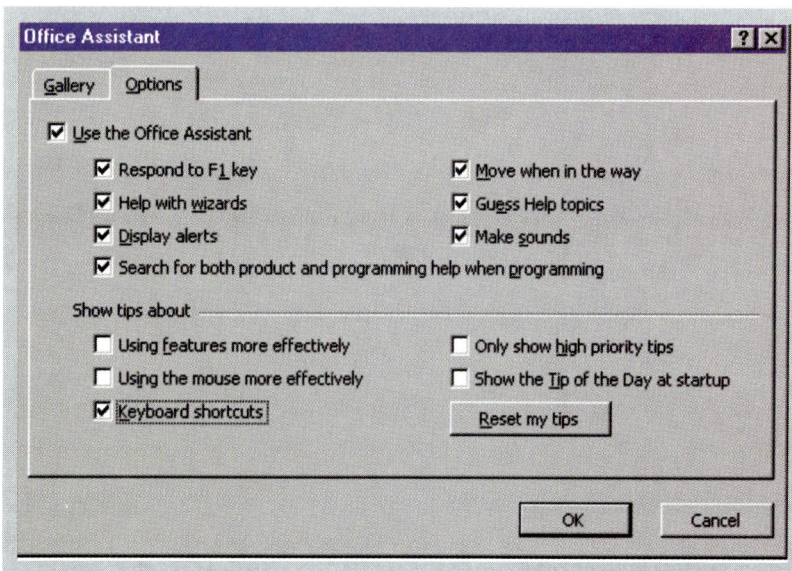

Practice

Open the student practice file, **Prac 1-1** and follow the directions.

Hot Tip

The Office Assistant is common to all Office 2000 applications. Therefore, any Assistant options you change will affect it in all Office programs.

Skill

Setting Up the Practice Inbox

Concept

During the exercises in Lesson 2, you will need to keep your actual e-mail messages separate from the practice e-mail created for the purpose of this book. To do this, you will create a practice Inbox for Virginia Reynolds.

Do It!

You will create a practice Inbox for VReynolds.

1 Click the Inbox Shortcut 📨 on the Outlook Bar.

2 If the Folder List is not displayed, click View on the Menu bar, then click Folder List. Your screen should now look similar to **Figure 1-12**.

3 Next to the New Mail Message button 🗋 New ▾ on the Standard toolbar is a drop down arrow. Click it, and then click the Folder command on the menu that opens.

4 In the Create New Folder dialog box that opens (**Figure 1-13**), check to be sure that Mail Items is displayed in the Folder Contains text box.

5 Type VReynolds Practice Inbox in the Name text box and click ❘ OK ❘.

6 When prompted to add a shortcut to the Outlook Bar, click ❘ No ❘. The Practice Inbox folder is now in the Folder List as a subfolder of the Inbox.

7 Click the 🗋 New ▾ drop-down arrow. Click Outlook Bar Shortcut. The Add to Outlook Bar dialog box will appear (**Figure 1-14**).

8 On the Folder List, you will see a plus sign (**+**) next to the Inbox. Click the plus sign to display the subfolder.

9 Click the VReynolds Practice Inbox folder.

10 Click ❘ OK ❘ in the Add to Outlook Bar dialog box. The VReynolds Practice Inbox shortcut 📨 is now on the Outlook Bar. Scroll down in the Outlook Bar if you cannot see it.

More

You can move a shortcut to a different location on the Outlook Bar by clicking and dragging. It is recommended that you click and drag the VReynolds Practice Inbox to just below the Inbox. To do so, click and drag the VReynolds Practice Inbox icon until the black bar is underneath the Inbox icon. Release the mouse button and the VReynolds Practice Inbox shortcut will be moved.

Figure 1-12 Outlook 2000 Folder List

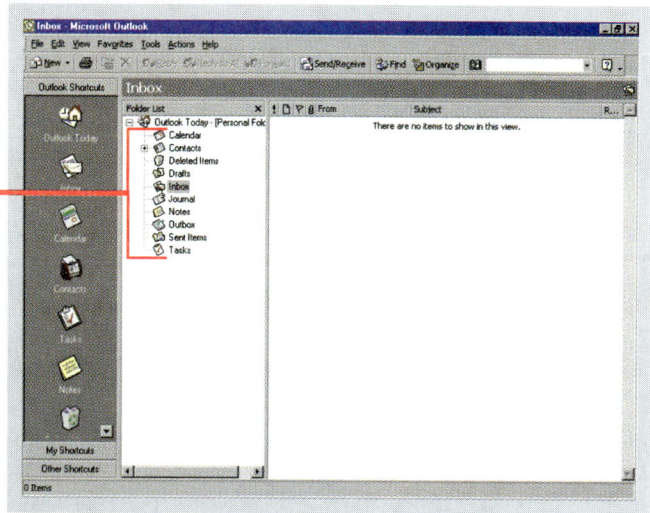

Folder List

Figure 1-13 Create New Folder dialog box

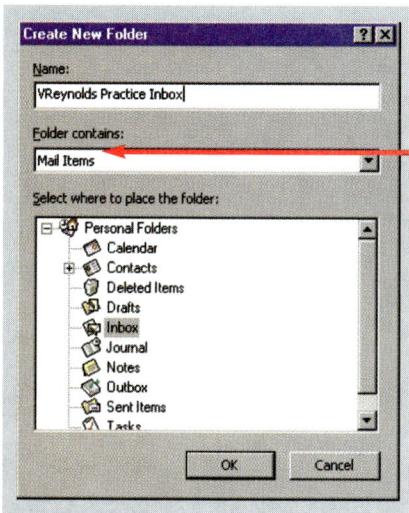

This label must be displayed in your Create New Folder dialog box

Figure 1-14 Add to Outlook Bar dialog box

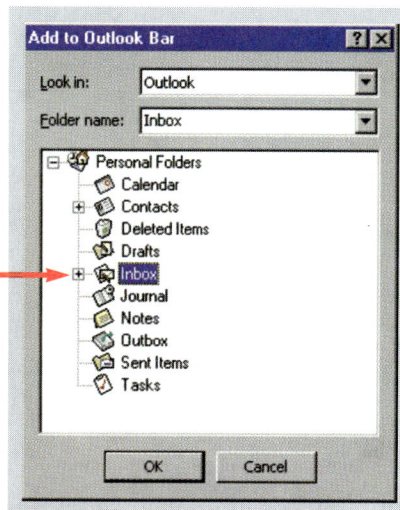

Click here

Hot Tip

By right-clicking a folder in the Folder List, you can quickly add a shortcut to the Outlook Bar. When the menu opens, click **Add to Outlook Bar**.

OL 1.11

Skill

Installing the Practice E-Mail Files

Concept

In the business world, e-mail will arrive and show up automatically in your Inbox. For the purposes of this book, however, you will not be working with real e-mail messages. You will use the practice files to do the exercises.

Do It!

You will locate and move the practice e-mail messages into your practice Inbox.

1. With the Outlook program on the screen and the VReynolds Practice Inbox open, click **Start** on the taskbar, select **Programs**, and select the **Windows Explorer** program that is on your computer. Explorer will open on top of the Outlook window (**Figure 1-15**).

2. Click the **drive icon** that contains the practice files.

3. Locate the **Practice E-Mail** folder. Double-click on it to open it.

4. Move the mouse pointer to the **Windows taskbar** and right-click on a blank area of it.

5. Click **Tile Vertically** or **Tile Windows Vertically**, depending on the version of Windows you are running. Your screen should look like **Figure 1-16**.

6. Click and drag the practice e-mail messages (the ones with the envelope icons) from the Practice E-mail Folder to the **VReynolds Practice Inbox** folder in the Folder List.

7. After the messages are transferred, click [X] in the Explorer window to close it.

8. Click the Maximize button [□] located in the upper-right of the Outlook screen to enlarge Outlook and make it fill the screen. Click [icon] on the Outlook Bar to see the practice e-mails. **DO NOT** open them at this time.

More

Once you have completed this book, you may wish to delete the shortcuts and practice files you have created. To delete the practice e-mail messages, highlight each one in the Messages window and press the [Delete] key. This will delete the message and send it to Deleted Items. To delete a shortcut, right-click the shortcut, and click **Remove from Outlook Bar** on the shortcut menu.

When you delete an item from an Outlook folder it is not actually removed. It is moved to the **Deleted Items** folder. To permanently delete items you must empty the Deleted Items folder. To select multiple items for deletion, press the [Ctrl] key as you click each one.

To quickly empty the Deleted Items folder, right-click it in the Folder List and select the **Empty "Deleted Items" Folder** command from the shortcut menu. The Empty "Deleted Items" Folder command is also on the Tools menu. To retrieve an accidentally deleted item, right-click it and select the **Move to Folder** command from the shortcut menu. The Move to Folder command is also on the Edit menu.

Figure 1-15 Windows Explorer and Practice Inbox

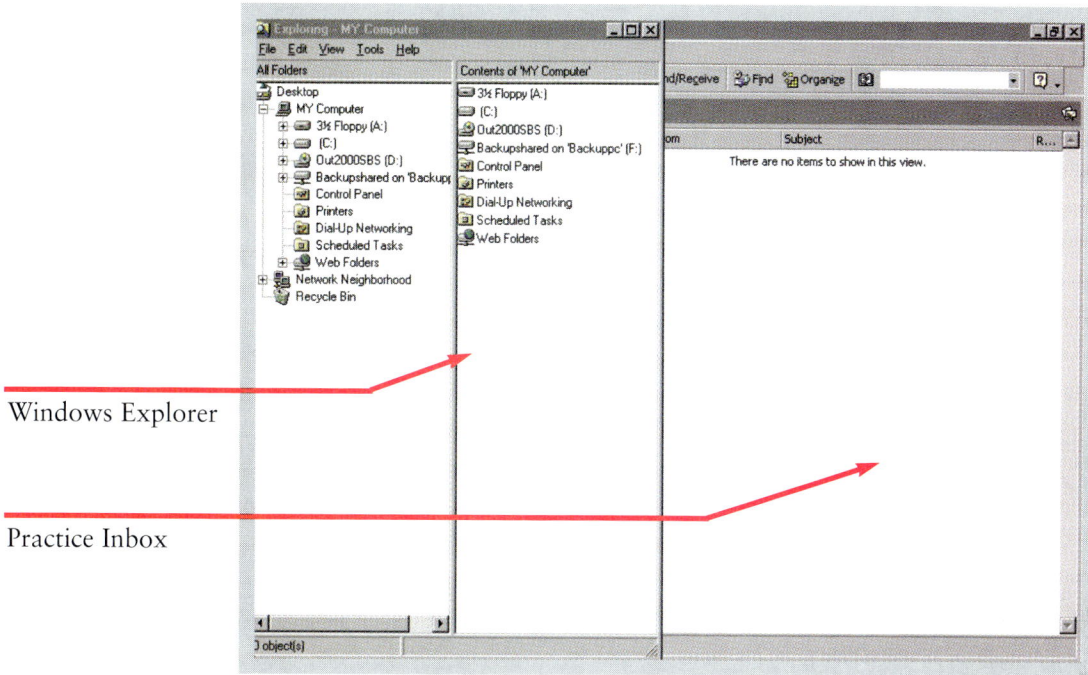

Windows Explorer

Practice Inbox

Figure 1-16 Practice e-mail and the VReynolds Practice Inbox

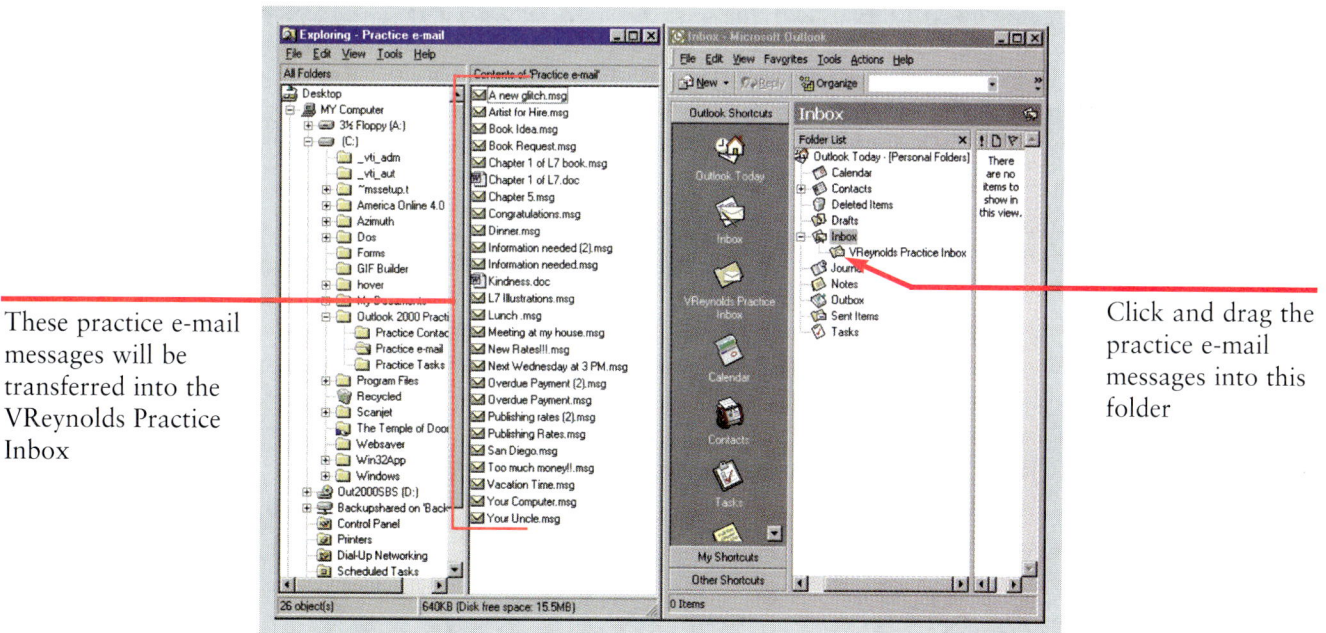

These practice e-mail messages will be transferred into the VReynolds Practice Inbox

Click and drag the practice e-mail messages into this folder

Hot Tip

To select all the practice e-mail messages at once, click on the first message, hold down the [**Shift**] key, and then click the last message. Now, you can click and drag the entire block to the Practice Inbox.

Skill

Installing the Practice Contacts Files

Concept

In the business world, you will be building your own files of contacts based on e-mails and other information that you receive. For the purposes of this book, however, we have developed some fictitious contacts for you. You will use these contacts to do the exercises.

Do It!

You will locate and move the practice contacts into your Contacts folder.

1 With the Outlook program on the screen and the Contacts section open, click **Start** on the taskbar, select Programs, and then click the Windows Explorer program that is on your computer. Explorer will open on top of the Calendar window (Figure 1-17).

2 Click the drive icon that contains the practice files.

3 Locate the Practice Contacts folder. Double-click on it to open it.

4 Move the mouse pointer to the Windows taskbar and right-click on a blank area of it.

5 Click Tile Vertically or Tile Windows Vertically, depending on the version of Windows you are running. Your screen should look like Figure 1-18.

6 Click and drag the practice contacts, the ones with the contact icons, from the Practice Contacts folder to the Contacts folder in the Folder List. (If the Folder List is not open, open the View menu, and click Folder List.)

7 After the contacts are transferred, click ✖ to close the Explorer window.

8 Click the Maximize button ▢ to maximize Outlook. Click the Contacts Shortcut icon in the Outlook Bar to view the practice contacts. DO NOT open them at this time.

More

Once you have completed this book, you may wish to delete the practice contacts. To do so, highlight each one in the Contacts window and press the [Delete] key. This will delete the contact and send it to the Deleted Items folder.

Figure 1-17 Windows Explorer and Contacts

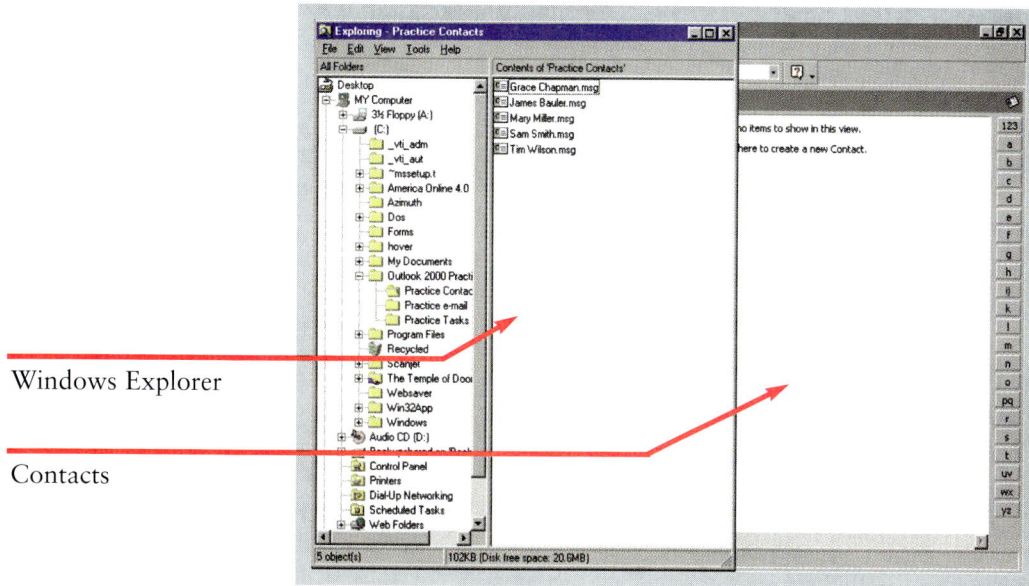

Windows Explorer

Contacts

Figure 1-18 Practice Contacts and Folder List

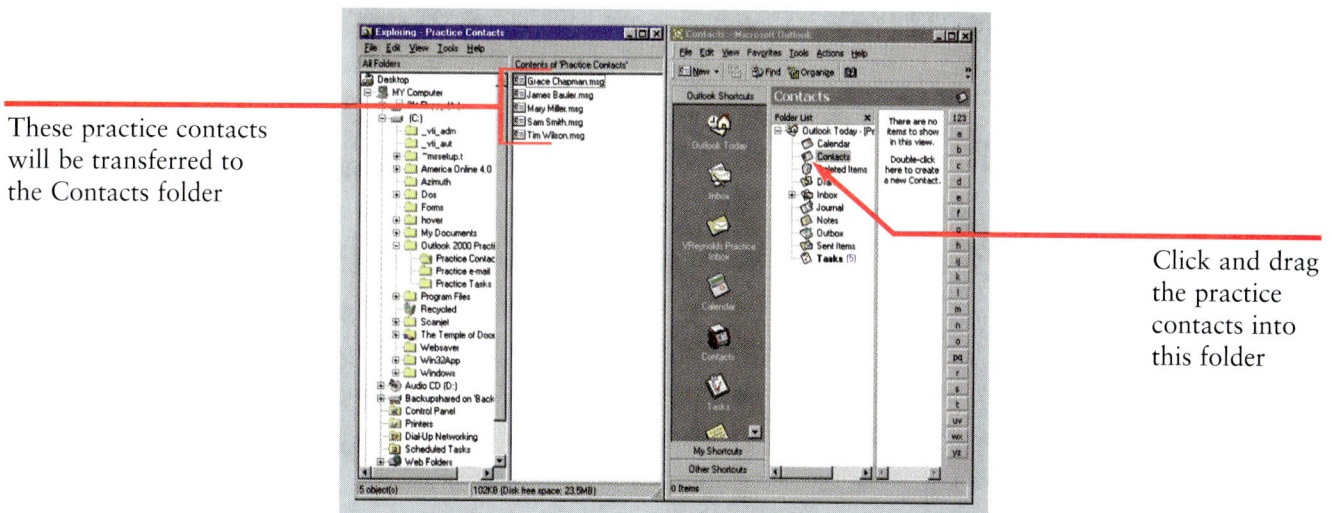

These practice contacts
will be transferred to
the Contacts folder

Click and drag
the practice
contacts into
this folder

Hot Tip

To select all the practice contacts at once,
click the first contact, hold down the
[Shift] key, and then click the last contact.
Now, you can click and drag the entire
block to the Contacts folder.

Shortcuts

Function	Button/Mouse	Menu	Keyboard
Outlook Today		Click View, select Go To, then click Outlook Today	[Alt V]+[G]+[K]
Calendar		Click View, select Go To, then click Calendar	[Alt V]+[G]+[C]
Inbox		Click View, select Go To, then click Inbox	[Ctrl]+[Shift]+[I]
New Mail Message	New	Click File, select New, then click Mail Message	[Ctrl]+[N]
VReynolds Practice Inbox			
Maximize a window		Click Control Icon, then click Maximize	
Close a window		Click Control icon, then click Close	
Office Assistant		Click Help, then click Microsoft Outlook Help	[F1]

Quiz

Identify Key Features

Name the items identified by callouts in **Figure 1-19**.

Figure 1-19 Elements of the Outlook Today screen

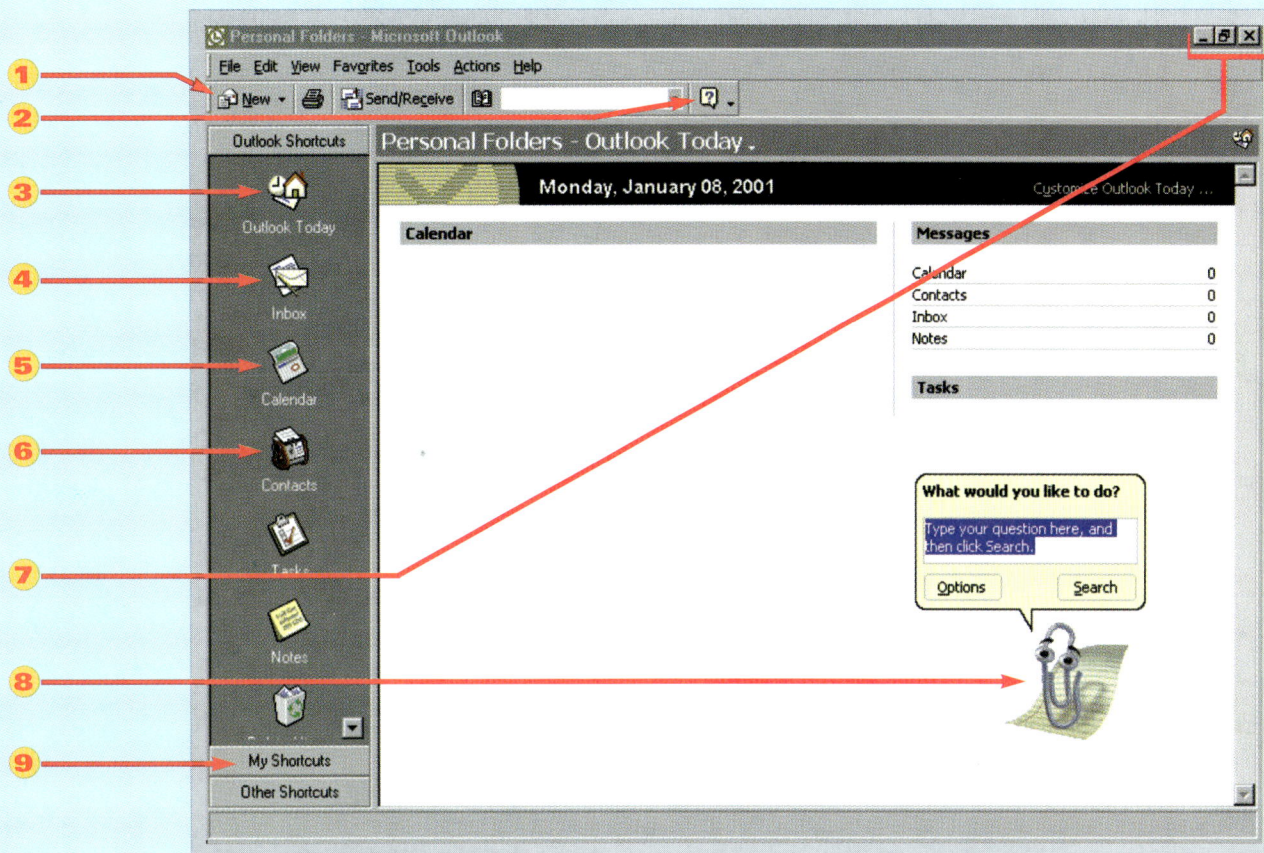

Select The Best Answer

10. Click this to make the Outlook window fill the screen

11. Displays shortcuts to all functions of Outlook 2000

12. Answers any questions you might have about Outlook 2000

13. Displays the shortcuts for Drafts, Outbox, Sent Items, Journal, and Outlook Update

14. Click this to go directly to your e-mail

a. Outlook Bar

b. Inbox icon

c. Maximize button

d. Office Assistant

e. My Shortcuts

Quiz (continued)

Complete the Statement

15. To see an overview of the Calendar, Messages, and Tasks all at once, click:

    a. Inbox

    b. Calendar

    c. Outlook Today

    d. My Shortcuts

16. To see the shortcut icon for My Documents, click:

    a. Outlook Today

    b. Outlook Shortcuts

    c. My Shortcuts

    d. Other Shortcuts

17. All of these are settings to customize Outlook Today, except:

    a. Standard (three column)

    b. Winter

    c. Summer

    d. Standard (one column)

18. To hide the Office Assistant, you should:

    a. Left-click on the Assistant, and click "Hide" from the menu

    b. Open the File menu, and click on "Go Away"

    c. Right-click on the Assistant and click "Hide" from the menu

    d. Click the Search button

19. You can move a shortcut to a different location on the Outlook Bar by:

    a. Clicking and dragging

    b. Copy and Paste

    c. Delete and rename

    d. Click and paste

20. To show two applications on the screen at the same time, right-click the Windows taskbar and select:

    a. Tile side by side

    b. Tile vertically

    c. Tile diagonally

    d. Tile the desktop

Interactivity

Test Your Skills

1. Open the Outlook application and navigate to the VReynolds Practice Inbox:
   a. Use the Start button to launch Microsoft Outlook.
   b. Scroll through the Outlook Bar until the VReynolds Practice Inbox shortcut is visible.
   c. Click the shortcut.

2. Add the Deleted Items folder to the Messages section of Outlook Today:
   a. Click Customize Outlook Today.
   b. Click Choose Folders.
   c. Click the check box for Deleted Items, then click OK.
   d. Click Save Changes.

3. Get help from the Office Assistant:
   a. Open the Office Assistant's dialog balloon.
   b. Ask the Assistant for information on how to customize toolbars.
   c. Choose a topic that the Assistant provides, and then read the information in the Help window.
   d. Close the Help window when you are done, and then close the Office Assistant's window.

4. Add VReynolds Practice Notes to the Notes section of Outlook.
   a. Click the Notes icon on the Outlook Bar.
   b. Click View on the Menu bar, then click Folder List.
   c. Click the down arrow next to the New Note button and select Folder.
   d. Type VReynolds Practice Notes in the Name text box and click OK.
   e. Click Yes when asked whether you would like to add a shortcut to the Outlook Bar.

Interactivity (continued)

Problem Solving

1. Assume that you have just accepted a position as a media consultant. Create two new Inboxes for this position. Label the first Inbox Professional Correspondence. Label the second Inbox Personal Correspondence. Add shortcuts for both Inboxes to the Other Shortcuts section of the Outlook Bar. Finally, customize the Outlook Today screen so that both Inboxes appear in the Messages section.

2. Due to a recent merger, your company is absorbing the responsibilities of another company. You realize that this means more work for everyone, however, you are elated with the opportunity to put Outlook 2000 to work. Your first job as the merger approaches is to create three new mailboxes for e-mail addresses which will be given to you at a later date. You do know, however, that the first mailbox is to handle business correspondence for Alzine Manufacturing. The second mailbox is a temporary one to handle the Human Resources department's e-mail. The third mailbox will accommodate correspondence specifically related to Public Relations. Create these three mailboxes.

3. Customize Outlook Today by applying a different visual setting. Also, add any folders not already in the Messages section.

LESSON

2

MANAGING E-MAIL

E-mail is a rapid and convenient form of communication. Prior to the advent of e-mail, businesses had only two communication choices: telephone or letters, delivered by the postal service, courier, or via fax machine. E-mail offers many advantages over telephones and letters. Any information given over the telephone must be written down or remembered for future reference. Furthermore, the person you are trying to contact has to be there to answer. Anyone who has ever played "phone tag" can attest to the unsatisfactory solution provided by answering devices and voice-mail systems. Using e-mail, your messages are received practically instantaneously. You can view your messages on your computer screen, save them indefinitely for referencing, print copies, send copies to colleagues, attach files, and insert Internet hyperlinks, all without losing information. With e-mail, recipients can be away from their offices and respond to your message when they return. Hard copy verification letters are no longer necessary and information will be received much sooner than other forms of letter delivery.

Nearly all businesses and professions recognize the advantages of e-mail. Learning to communicate by e-mail and how to manage and organize your e-mail files is an essential business skill. In this lesson you will learn how to open and print e-mail and open e-mail attachments that are sent to you. Next, you will learn how to send, reply to, forward, and recall e-mail. You will also learn how to add a signature block, use the Outlook 2000 Address Book, locate messages on a particular subject, and use a template to give your e-mail a distinctive stationery look. Finally, you will learn how to sort and archive your messages to maintain an organized and efficient communication system.

Case Study:
In this lesson Virginia will use Outlook 2000's e-mail features. She will open and read e-mail, as well as send it. She will reply to, forward, and recall e-mail. She will learn how to customize e-mail by adding a signature and using mail templates. Finally, she will learn some advanced techniques for e-mail: using the Address Book, finding messages, sorting mail, and setting viewing options.

E-Mail Basics

Concept

Since e-mail is fast becoming the preferred choice for business communications, it is important to know how to open, print, and navigate within the e-mail you receive.

Do It!

Virginia will open and print an e-mail.

1. If the Practice e-mail messages are not installed in the VReynolds Practice Inbox, you should install them before continuing. Follow the instructions in Lesson 1 for installing the practice files.

2. Click the VReynolds Practice Inbox shortcut that you created. The inbox will open and contain the practice e-mails you moved earlier.

3. Double-click the e-mail from Sam Smith entitled L7 Illustrations (see Figure 2-1). A separate window opens showing you the e-mail. Read the e-mail.

4. Since Virginia is new to Outlook, she does not have her supervisor's e-mail address. Therefore, she must print this e-mail to show to him.

5. Open the File menu on the Message window's Menu bar. When the menu opens, click Print. The Print dialog box opens (Figure 2-2).

6. Click Page Setup....

7. When the Page Setup: Memo Style dialog box opens, click Font... in the Title section

8. The Font dialog box opens. Click Times New Roman to select it.

9. Click OK to close the Font dialog box.

10. Click OK in the Page Setup: Memo Style dialog box.

11. Click OK in the Print dialog box to print the e-mail.

12. Click the Close button ⊠ on the Message window's Title bar.

More

Outlook 2000 can be customized to notify you when new e-mail arrives. To activate this feature, open the Tools menu, and click Options. In the Options dialog box, click on the Preferences tab. Click the E-Mail Options button. In the Message Handling section, click the check box for Display a Notification Message when New Mail Arrives. Click the OK buttons to close both dialog boxes. The option is now active and you will be notified when you receive new mail.

Figure 2-1 E-mail from Sam Smith

Title bar

Menu bar

Standard toolbar

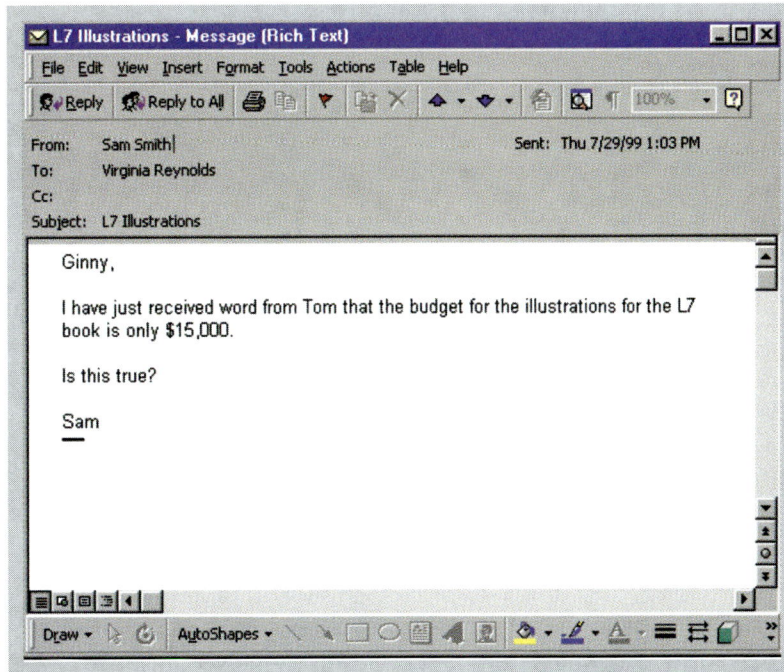

Figure 2-2 Print dialog box

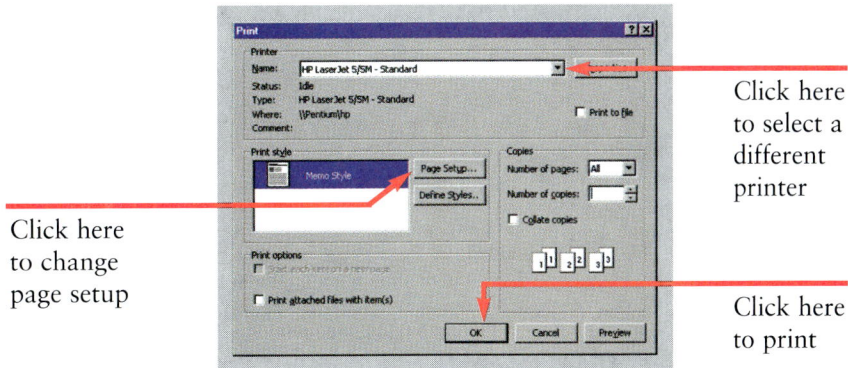

Click here to select a different printer

Click here to change page setup

Click here to print

Practice

Open the student practice file, **Prac 2-1** and follow the directions.

Hot Tip

If you do not need to make any changes to the format of an e-mail before printing it, you can print the e-mail immediately by clicking on the **Print** button on the **Message window's Standard toolbar**.

Working with Attachments

Skill

Concept

E-mail can be sent with attachments containing documents, graphics, movies, or sound files that are either too large to fit in the main body of the e-mail or are formatted differently. E-mail with an attachment is marked in the Inbox with a paper clip icon. You must have a program installed on your computer that is compatible with the attached file to open the attachment. Attachments often contain supporting documentation that you will need to open and save for later use.

Do It!

Virginia will open an e-mail with an attachment and save the attachment.

1 If the VReynolds Practice Inbox is not open, click 📧 on the Outlook Bar to open it.

2 Double-click the e-mail from Mary Miller. The mail opens and an attachment icon 📄 is displayed at the bottom of the Message window as shown in **Figure 2-3**.

3 Double-click the 📄 icon. A dialog box (Opening Mail Attachment) may appear.

4 If the dialog box does appear, click the Open It radio button. Click OK . The attachment will open in Microsoft Word. If you do not have Microsoft Word, however, it will open in Microsoft WordPad.

5 From this point, you can print the attachment, make changes to it, or save it.

6 Open the File menu and click Save As.

7 The Save As dialog box opens (**Figure 2-4**). Select a folder to place the attachment in. We recommend placing it in the My Documents folder.

8 Select the current file name in the File name text box, and type Chapter 1 of L7 by MMiller.

9 Click the 💾 Save button.

10 Click ❌ on Microsoft Word or WordPad to close it.

11 Click ❌ on the Message window's Title bar to close it.i

More

You now have two copies of the attachment on your computer. One is saved in the My Documents folder (or whichever one you picked), and the other is still attached to the original e-mail. If you delete the e-mail before opening the attachment, the attachment will be deleted along with the e-mail, but the file you saved in My Documents will still be available. You can save several attachments in the same folder by opening the File menu, highlighting Save Attachments, and selecting the All Attachments command.

Figure 2-3 E-mail Message with attachment

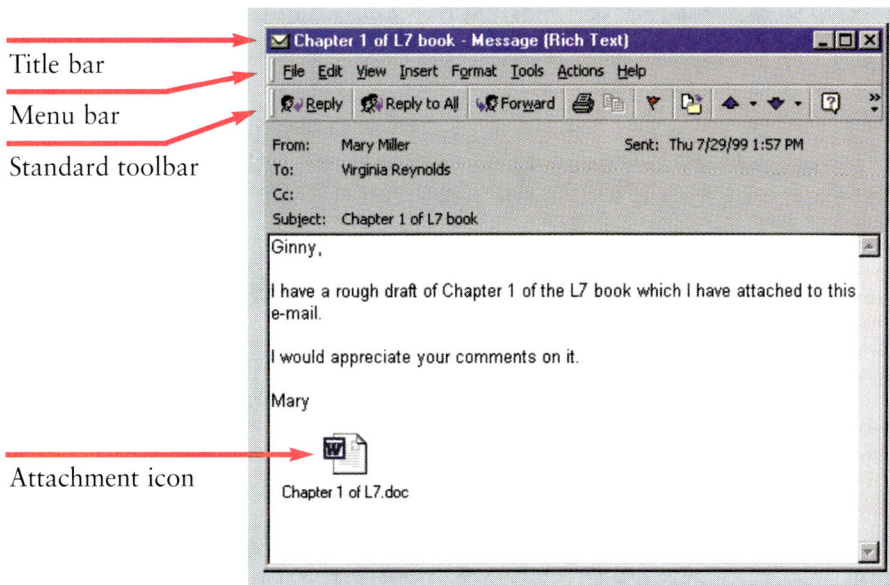

Title bar

Menu bar

Standard toolbar

Attachment icon

Figure 2-4 Save As dialog box

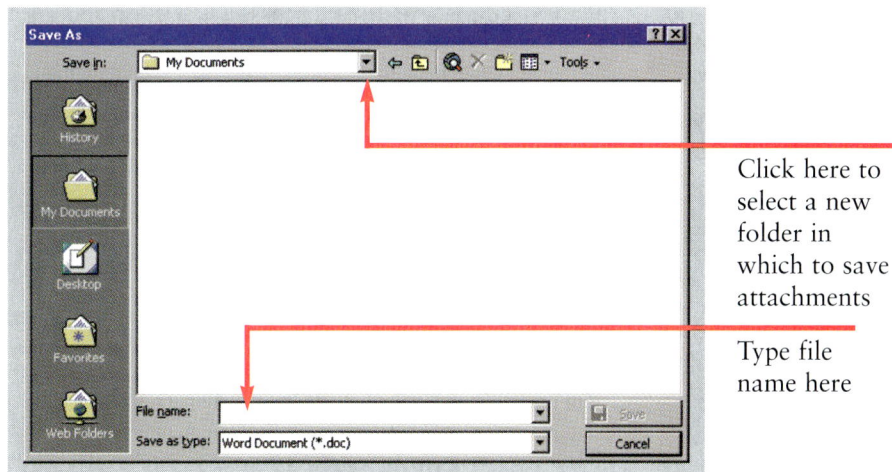

Click here to
select a new
folder in
which to save
attachments

Type file
name here

Practice

Open the student practice file, **Prac 2-2**
and follow the directions.

Hot Tip

To save an attachment without opening it,
right-click the **Attachment icon**. When the
shortcut menu appears, click **Save As**.

Skill

Sending E-Mail

Concept

E-mail messages can be used to communicate with co-workers, customers, suppliers, advertisers, and any other business and personal contacts you may have. It is fast, efficient and costs less than a phone call. Outlook 2000 makes it simple and convenient to compose, address, and send e-mail.

Do It!

Virginia has been given the e-mail address of an artist who provides illustrations for Poorman's Press. She has been told to contact the artist regarding his availability to work on a new project.

1. If it is not open, open the VReynolds Practice Inbox by clicking 📧 on the Outlook Bar.

2. Click the New Mail Message button 🔲 New ▾ on the left side of the Standard toolbar. A blank Message form opens (**Figure 2-5**), with the default name Untitled and with the cursor blinking in the To: text box.

3. Type Mwilson@artist.artist.

4. Press the [Tab] key to go to the next line. This is the CC or Courtesy Copy text box. Using this box, you can send copies of this e-mail to others. Since there is no one to CC this e-mail to, press the [Tab] key again.

5. In the Subject text box, type Your Availability. Press the [Tab] Key.

6. Type the following in the Message text box:
   Mike,

   We have a new book to illustrate in the L7 series. Would you be available to do the artwork?

   Sincerely, Ginny

7. Your e-mail should now look like **Figure 2-6**.

8. Click the Send button 🔲 Send on the Message form's Standard toolbar to send the e-mail.

More

During these lessons, you will be sending e-mails to fictitious addresses. If your computer is connected to a server, Outlook will send the e-mail and you will receive a reply stating that the e-mail was undeliverable. Ignore these messages.

If you send your e-mail through your company's network, or are using the Internet Only configuration and are connected to the Internet, your message will be sent automatically when you click the Send button. If you are not currently connected to the Internet, your messages will be placed in the Outbox. To send messages in the Outbox, Open the Outlook Today Information viewer, click the Send/Receive button 🔲 Send/Receive on the Standard toolbar and complete the instructions from your ISP (Internet Service Provider) to access the Internet.

Figure 2-5 Blank Message form

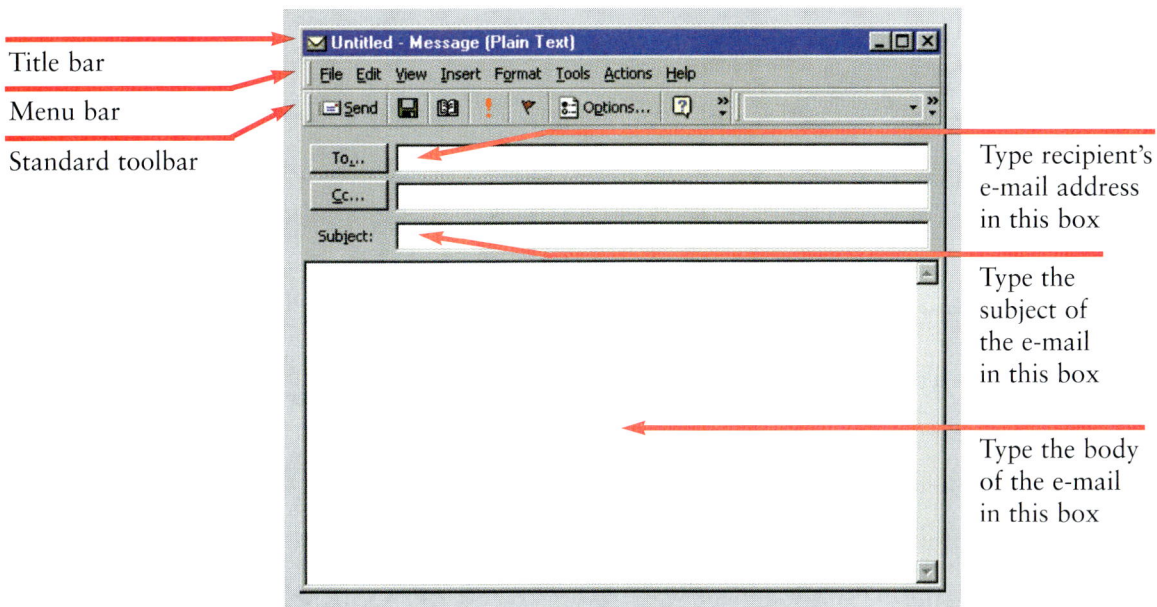

Title bar

Menu bar

Standard toolbar

Type recipient's
e-mail address
in this box

Type the
subject of
the e-mail
in this box

Type the body
of the e-mail
in this box

Figure 2-6 Completed Message form

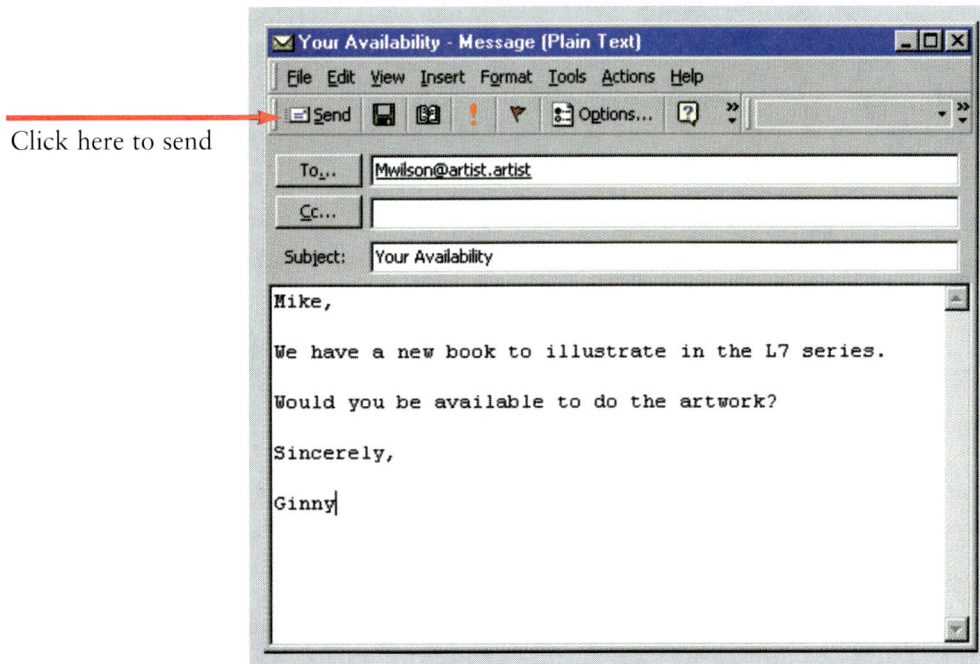

Click here to send

Practice

Open the student practice file, **Prac 2-3** and follow the directions.

Hot Tip

There are several keyboard shortcuts available in the Outlook program to write and send mail. Pressing **[Ctrl]+[N]** will automatically open a blank Message form. Pressing **[Ctrl]+[Enter]** will send the message.

Skill   Replying to E-Mail

Concept

Outlook 2000 provides several different ways to reply to e-mail that you receive: Reply, Reply to All, and Forward. When you use Reply (as well as Reply to All), the original message is copied onto the reply. This enables the recipients to remember and view the information you are referring to, thus keeping communications clear and understandable. It also provides substantiation for business transactions.

Do It!

Virginia will read and reply to two e-mails.

1 If it is not open, open the **VReynolds Practice Inbox** by clicking 🖹 on the Outlook Bar.

2 Open the e-mail from **William Sampson** entitled **Lunch?**.

3 After reading the e-mail, click the **Reply** button 🔲Reply on the **Message form's** Standard toolbar. A **Reply form**, with the title **RE: Lunch?** in the Message form's Title bar and Subject text box, appears, addressed to William Sampson . An insertion point appears in the Message text box, just above a copy of the message to which you are replying (**Figure 2-7**).

4 Type **Bill, Absolutely. I've got some great new ideas. Ginny**. Click 🔲Send .

5 Click ❎ on the original Message form's Title bar.

6 Open the e-mail from **Sam Smith** entitled **Meeting At My House**.

7 After reading the e-mail, click **Reply to All** 🔲Reply to All on the Message form's Standard toolbar. The Reply form appears with **Sam Smith** and **Virginia Reynolds** in the **To:** text box and several names in the **Cc:** box (**Figure 2-8**).

8 Type: **Sorry, gang. I have to miss this meeting. Ginny**. Click 🔲Send .

9 Click ❎ on the original Message form's Title bar. The message now appears in the Inbox with an open envelope icon showing a small red arrow 🔲 . This icon indicates that you have read and replied to this e-mail.

More

If you want to Reply to All, but do not want to reveal the e-mail addresses of the other recipients, click the **Cc** button in the Message form. In the **Select Names** dialog box, delete the names in the Cc list box. Transfer them from the **Contact** list to the **Bcc** (Blind Courtesy Copy) list box, using the Bcc button 🔲Bcc-> . The e-mail message header will not show the recipient's names or e-mail addresses.

Figure 2-7 RE: Lunch? Reply form

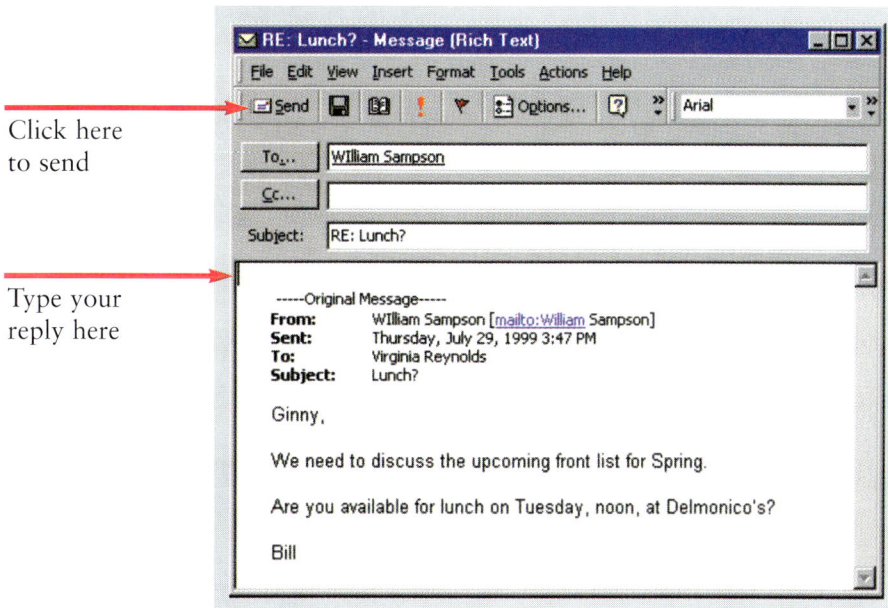

Click here
to send

Type your
reply here

RE: Lunch? - Message (Rich Text)

File Edit View Insert Format Tools Actions Help

Send | | | | | Options... | | Arial

To...   WIlliam Sampson

Cc...

Subject: RE: Lunch?

    -----Original Message-----
From: WIlliam Sampson [mailto:William Sampson]
Sent: Thursday, July 29, 1999 3:47 PM
To: Virginia Reynolds
Subject: Lunch?

Ginny,

We need to discuss the upcoming front list for Spring.

Are you available for lunch on Tuesday, noon, at Delmonico's?

Bill

Figure 2-8 RE: Meeting at my house Reply form

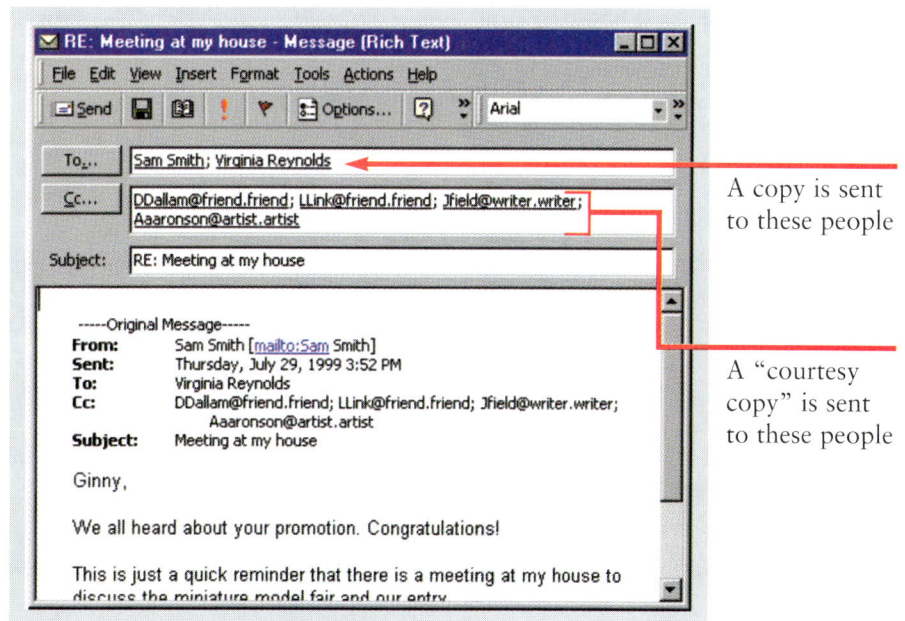

RE: Meeting at my house - Message (Rich Text)

File Edit View Insert Format Tools Actions Help

Send | | | | | Options... | | Arial

To...   Sam Smith; Virginia Reynolds

Cc...   DDallam@friend.friend; LLink@friend.friend; Jfield@writer.writer;
         Aaaronson@artist.artist

Subject: RE: Meeting at my house

    -----Original Message-----
From: Sam Smith [mailto:Sam Smith]
Sent: Thursday, July 29, 1999 3:52 PM
To: Virginia Reynolds
Cc: DDallam@friend.friend; LLink@friend.friend; Jfield@writer.writer;
               Aaaronson@artist.artist
Subject: Meeting at my house

Ginny,

We all heard about your promotion. Congratulations!

This is just a quick reminder that there is a meeting at my house to
discuss the miniature model fair and our entry.

A copy is sent
to these people

A "courtesy
copy" is sent
to these people

Practice

Open the student practice file, **Prac 2-4** and follow the directions.

Hot Tip

Instead of using the Reply button on the Standard toolbar, you can use **[Ctrl]+[R]** to generate a Reply form.

Skill

Forwarding E-Mail

Concept

There will be times when an e-mail you receive needs to be sent on to another individual. It may contain pertinent information for a co-worker, or may refer to a project that has been reassigned. You could cut and paste the contents of the e-mail to a a new message form, but that is not the most efficient way. The most efficient way is to forward the e-mail.

Do It!

Virginia will open an e-mail from a potential artist and then forward it to her supervisor.

1 If it is not open, open the VReynolds Practice Inbox by clicking 📩 on the Outlook Bar.

2 Open the e-mail from Sarah Engles entitled Artist for Hire. Read the message.

3 Click the Forward button 📧 Forward on the Message form's Standard toolbar. The Forward Message form will appear with the title FW: Artist for Hire in the Subject text box (**Figure 2-9**).

4 Type Jbauler@boss.boss in the To: text box. Press the [Tab] key three times.

5 In the Message text box, type the reason for forwarding the e-mail:

> Boss:
> I know this artist and she is very good. I think she would be an asset to our staff.
> Ginny

6 Your e-mail should look like **Figure 2-10**.

7 Click 📧 Send .

8 Click ✖ on the Message form's Title bar.

More

You can forward a message to more than one person. If you are manually inserting the addresses, you must separate each address with a semicolon. You can also forward multiple messages at the same time, but they will be sent as attachments. Hold down the [Ctrl] key as you select each message you want to forward.

Forwarded messages appear in the Inbox with an open envelope icon showing a small blue arrow 📨 .

Figure 2-9 Forward Message form

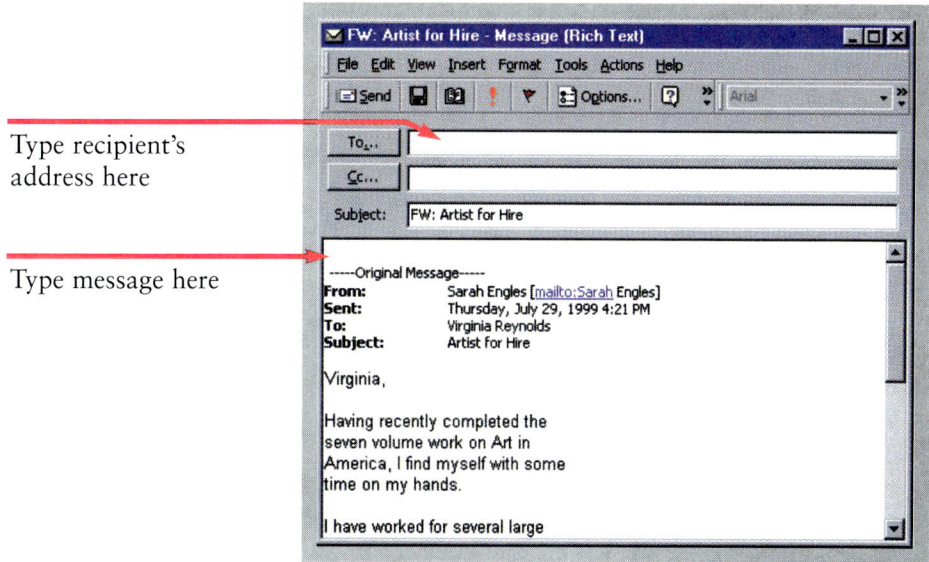

Type recipient's
address here

Type message here

Figure 2-10 Completed Forward Message form

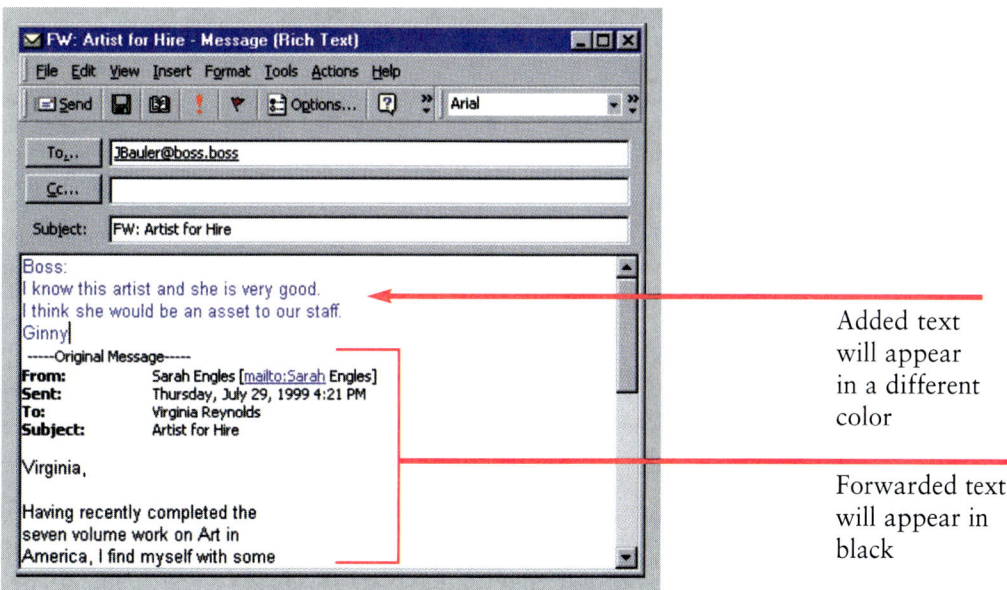

Added text
will appear
in a different
color

Forwarded text
will appear in
black

Practice

Open the student practice file, **Prac 2-5**
and follow the directions.

Hot Tip

You can forward any e-mail without reading it by highlighting the e-mail and clicking
the **Forward** button on the Message form's
Standard toolbar.

Skill **Recalling E-Mail**

Concept

Mistakes inevitably happen in the business world. Occasionally, you will send an e-mail out before it is complete, or with the wrong information. If this happens, Outlook has a feature that, subject to certain conditions, allows you to recall the e-mail before it is read.

Do It!

Virginia will recall an e-mail that was mistakenly sent to her supervisor.

1. If it is not open, open the VReynolds Practice Inbox by clicking 📧 on the Outlook Bar.

2. If the Folder List is not visible, click the View menu and then click Folder List.

3. Click the Sent Items folder in the Folder List. The Sent Items folder opens and will look similar to **Figure 2-11**.

4. Double-click the e-mail to Jbauler@boss.boss.

5. Open the Actions menu on the Message form's Standard toolbar and click Recall This Message.

6. The Recall This Message dialog box opens.

7. Click the Delete unread copies of this message radio button in the Are you sure you want to area of the Recall this Message dialog box. Click ⬛ OK ⬛ .

8. Click ❎ to close the original e-mail.

More

E-mail can only be recalled if the person to whom it was sent has not read it or moved it out of his or her Inbox. Furthermore, the recipient must have Outlook running, and the recipient's mail server must support the recall feature. So, don't count on being able to recall an errant message. However, if you do want to try, act quickly to increase your chances of success.

If you want to replace the original message, click the Delete unread copies and replace with a new message radio button. Edit the original message and click ⬛ Send . The new message will only be sent if the old message was successfully recalled.

If you have left the Tell Me If Recall Succeeds or Fails For Each Recipient check box in the Recall this Message dialog box checked, Outlook will notify you

Figure 2-11 Sent Items Folder

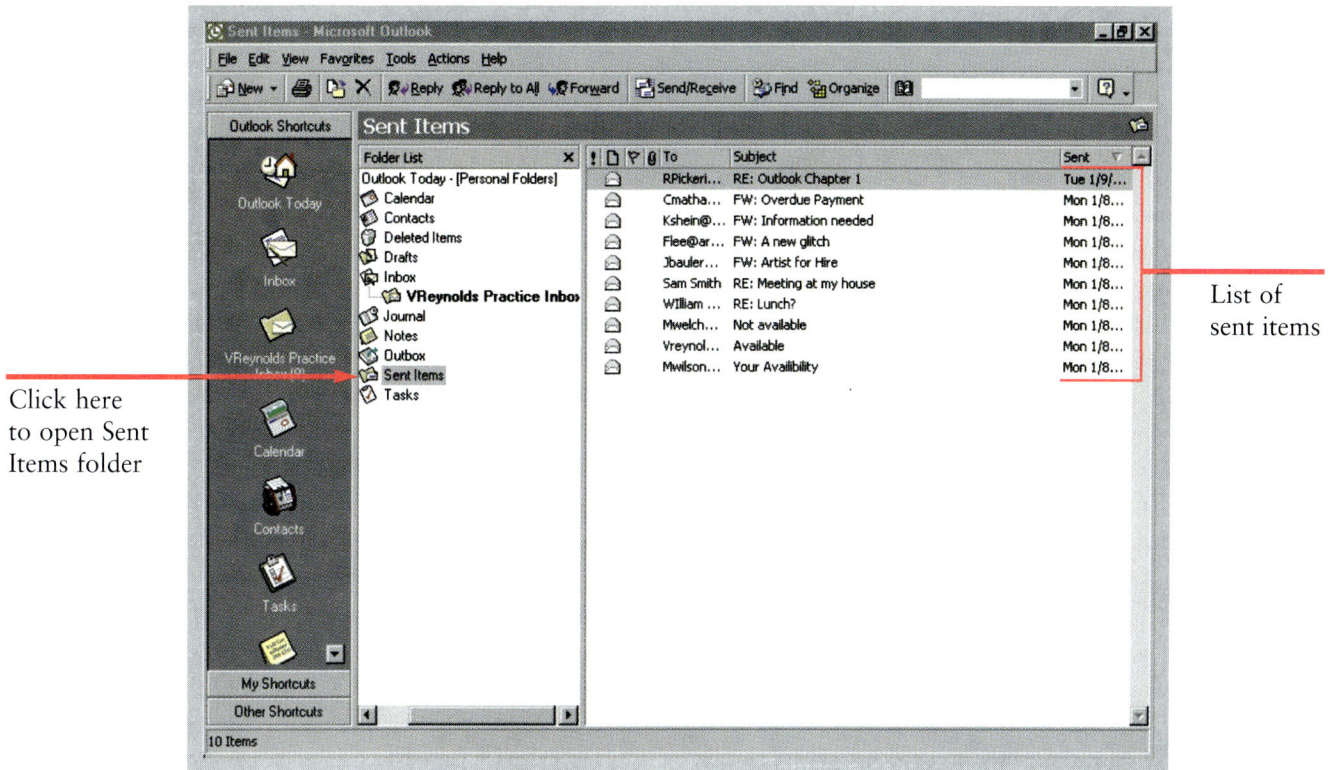

Click here
to open Sent
Items folder

List of
sent items

Practice

Recall any three e-mails of your choice
from the VReynolds Practice Inbox.

Hot Tip

Pressing **[Ctrl]+[Enter]** is the shortcut for
sending an e-mail in an Internet Only environment. Otherwise, you must use the
Send button.

Skill

Adding a Signature to E-Mail

Concept

One of the time-saving features of Outlook is the Signature option. Using this option, you can create an electronic signature that will add your name and contact information to all new messages. A signature block can contain your name, address, title, company name and any additional information you want to include. Multiple signatures can be created for business or personal use.

Do It!

Virginia will create a signature for her e-mail.

1. With the VReynolds Practice Inbox open, open the Tools menu and select Options.

2. Click the Mail Format tab when the Options dialog box opens (**Figure 2-12**).

3. Make sure the Use Microsoft Word to Edit E-mail Messages checkbox is not checked.

4. Click the Signature Picker button in the Signature area.

5. In the Signature Picker dialog box (**Figure 2-13**), click New... . The Create New Signature dialog box opens.

6. In the Enter a Name For Your New Signature text box, type Business Signature. Click Next. The Edit Signature dialog box opens.

7. Type the following information:

   Virginia Reynolds
   Production Coordinator
   Poorman's Press
   1254 S. Dixie Highway
   Lantana, FL 33456
   561.555.4587

8. The Edit Signature dialog box should now look like **Figure 2-14**.

9. Click the Finish button Finish , and then click OK in the Signature Picker dialog box and the Options dialog box.

10. Click New . A blank Message form opens with the new signature already inserted.

11. Address the e-mail to Kwilliam@friend.friend. Press the [Tab] key three times.

12. Type the following:
    Kay,

    This is my new signature. What do you think?

Figure 2-12 Options dialog box

Click here

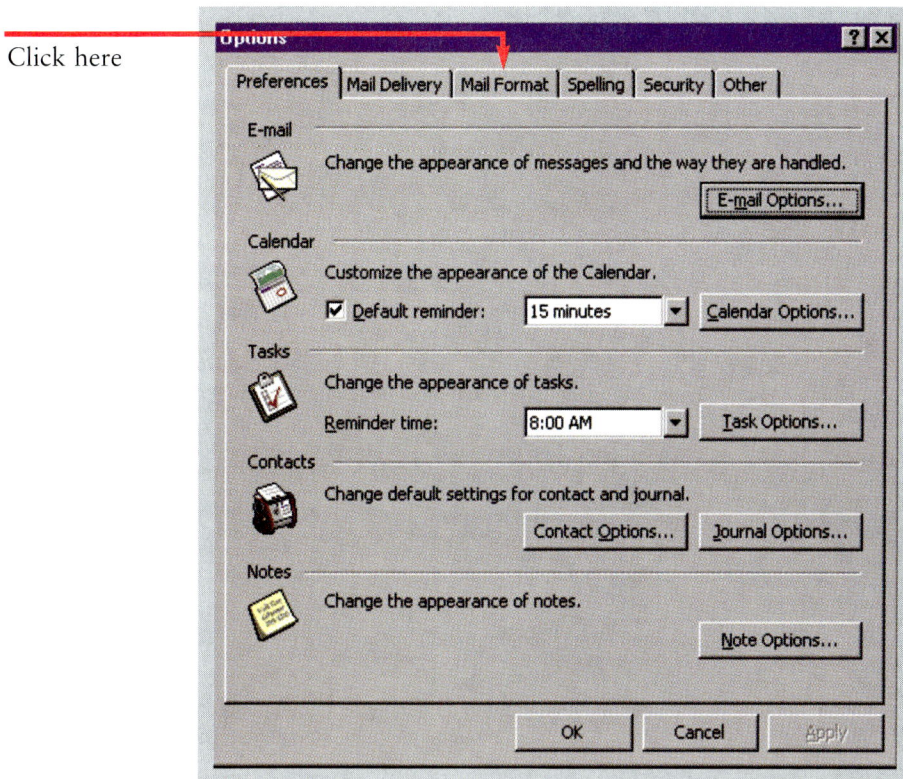

Figure 2-13 Signature Picker dialog box

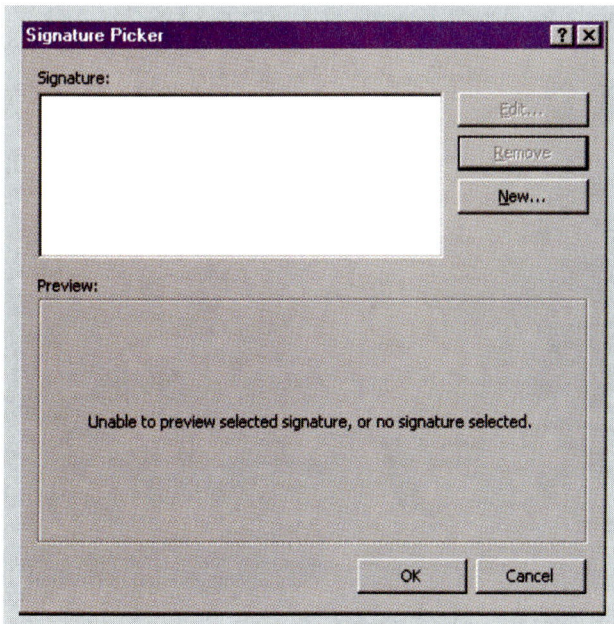

Figure 2-14 Edit Signature dialog box

Adding a Signature to Mail (continued)

Do It!

13 Your e-mail should look similar to **Figure 2-15**.

14 Click [Send] .

More

To edit a signature, reopen the Options dialog box on the Mail Format tab. In the Send in this message format list box, select Plain Text, Microsoft Outlook Rich Text or HTML format. Click the Signature Picker button. Select the signature you want to edit in the Signature box. Click the Edit button to open the Edit Signature dialog box. Edit the text in the Signature text box. Click the Font button to change the font, font style, size or effects. Click the Paragraph button to change the alignment of the signature block or apply bullets.

The Font and Paragraph buttons will only be enabled if you choose HTML or Microsoft Outlook Rich Text in the Message format section of the Options dialog box. These formatting options will not be available if you choose plain text as your message format. When the Font button is enabled, you can make your name slightly larger and boldfaced, or change the font color and italicize your address.

Multiple signature can be created by clicking the Signature Picker button and then the New button in the Signature Picker dialog box. To insert a signature in all your e-mail messages, open the Tools menu and select the Options command. On the Mail Format tab, select a signature from the Use this Signature by Default list box.

If you format your signatures using Rich Text or HTML formatting, when you send e-mail containing a signature block you may receive a warning message in the Plain Text Recipient Warning dialog box. It will advise you that some recipients may prefer to receive plain text messages, and ask you to confirm that you want to send the message in RTF or HTML format.

To stop using a signature, select <None> from the Use this signature by default list box. Then, if you want to insert a signature into an individual e-mail, open the Insert menu on the Message form's Standard toolbar. Highlight Signature and select the signature you want to use from the submenu. Click the More command to open the Select a Signature dialog box and view the signatures that are not listed on the Signature submenu.

To remove a signature just from the message you are currently composing, select the signature and press the [Delete] on the keyboard.

Figure 2-15 Completed e-mail

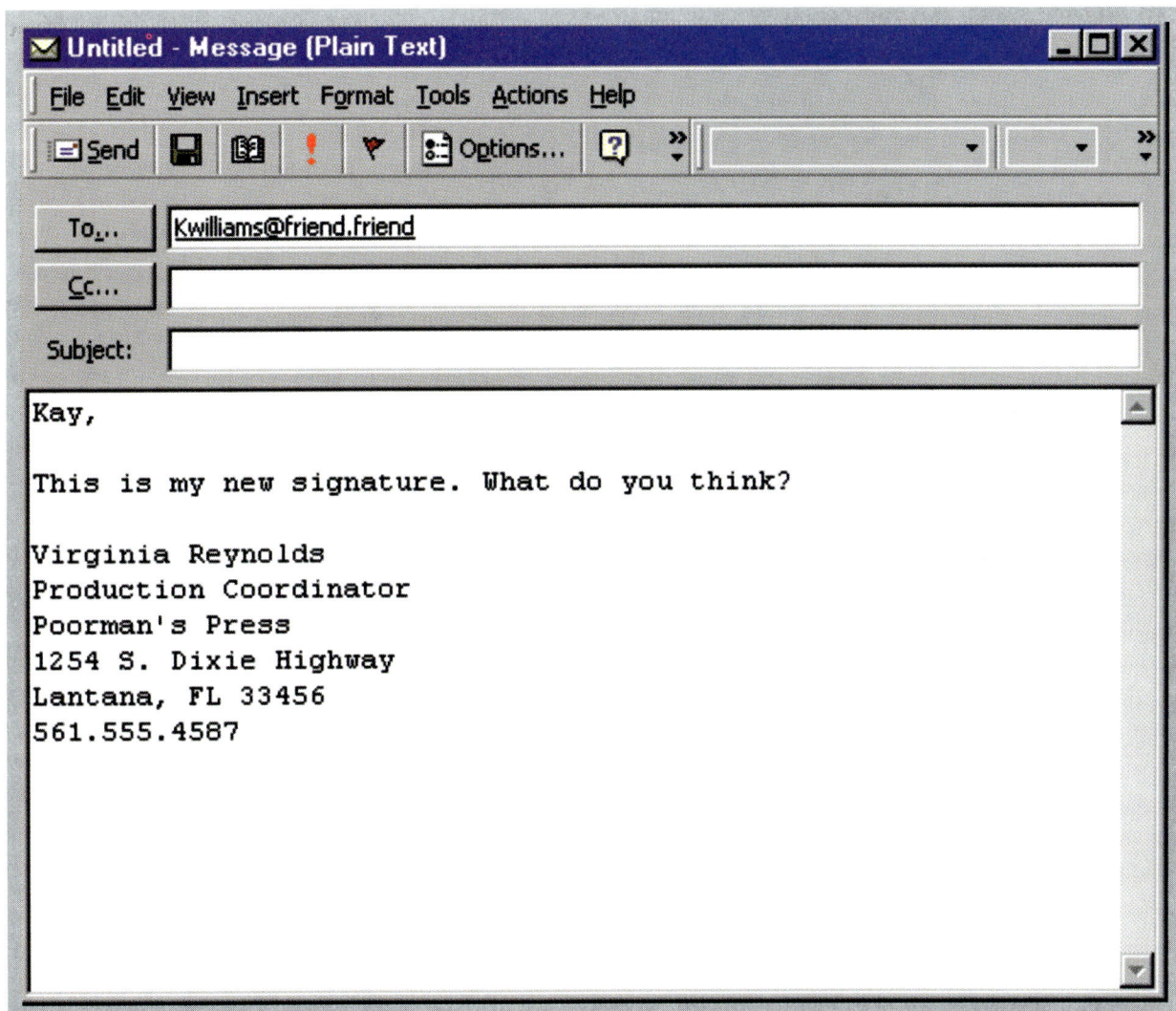

Practice

Create a personal signature for Virginia based on the following information. Ginny Reynolds lives at **124 Bullet Road** in **West Palm Beach, Florida**. Her apartment number is **12C** and the zip code is **33454**.

Hot Tip

In the Signature section of the Mail Format tab, there is a check box that states: **Don't use when replying or forwarding**. If it is checked, only new e-mail will have your signature. If unchecked, then all e-mail will bear your signature.

Skill

Using the Outlook Address Book

Concept

The Outlook Address Book in Outlook is a system for keeping track of those individuals who you contact on a regular basis. The Outlook Address Book can store a variety of information about each individual including private information such as birth date and the names of the addressee's children. Learning to use the Outlook Address Book will save you time when contacting people, and you will be less likely to lose addresses and phone numbers.

Do It!

Virginia will enter a name and e-mail address into the Outlook Address Book, and use the Address Book to address mail. NOTE: If you use Outlook 2000 with the Internet Only option or the No E-mail configuration, some of your screens may look different than those pictured.

1. Open the VReynolds Practice Inbox by clicking ✉ on the Outlook Bar.

2. Click the Address Book button ▣ on the Standard toolbar. The Address Book will open (**Figure 2-16**).

3. Click the New Entry button ▭ on the Address Book dialog box. The New Entry dialog box opens.

4. Select New Contact from the Select the Entry Type list box. Click ⬛ OK ⬛ .

5. A blank Contact form appears, with the default name Untitled, as shown in **Figure 2-17**. Type Mark James Roberts in the Full Name box.

6. Press the [Enter] key. The contact name is automatically entered as Roberts, Mark James in the File As list box.

7. Click the E-mail box and type Mroberts@roberts.roberts as the e-mail address.

8. Click the 🖫 Save and Close button. The Contact form closes and Mr. Roberts is added to your Contact list.

9. In the Outlook Address Book, click once on Jon Walter's name.

10. Click the Actions button ▣Action in the Address Book. From the submenu that opens, click Send Mail. A Message form opens, already addressed to Jon Walters.

11. Type By the 15th as the subject of the e-mail. In the Message text box, type Jon, Need the cover by the 15th. Click ▣ Send .

More

Once names are entered into the Outlook Address Book along with their appropriate e-mail addresses, you no longer have to type out the complete e-mail address for that person. You can simply type in the name, as it was entered into the Address Book and Outlook will automatically insert the e-mail address for you.

Figure 2-16 Outlook Address Book

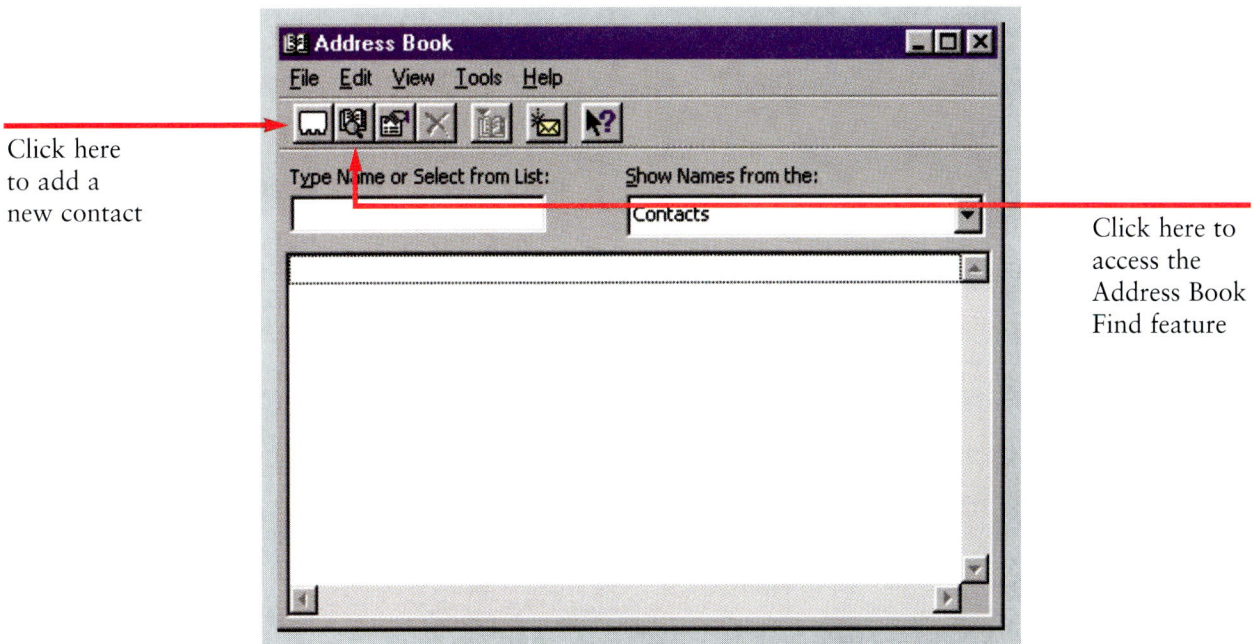

Click here to add a new contact

Click here to access the Address Book Find feature

Figure 2-17 Blank Contact form

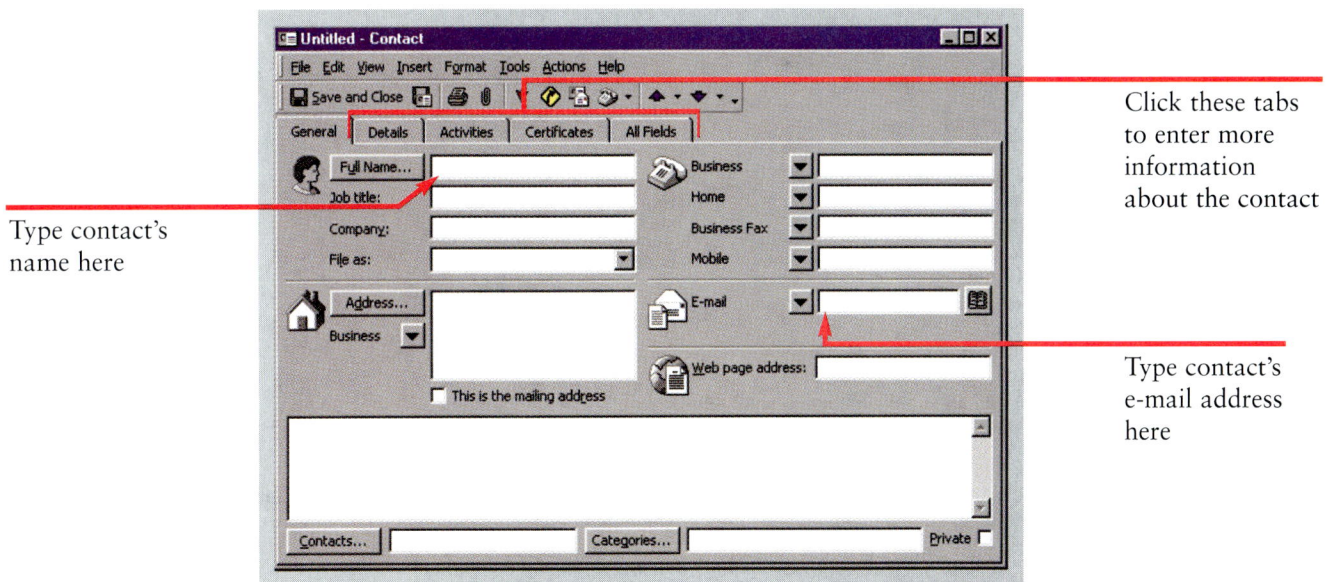

Click these tabs to enter more information about the contact

Type contact's name here

Type contact's e-mail address here

Practice

Open the student practice file, **Prac 2-6** and follow the directions.

Hot Tip

To quickly add information to an Address Book entry, simply type the last name in the **Find a Contact** box on the Standard toolbar of the Inbox and press **[Enter]**. Outlook will find and open the Address Book entry for that person.

Skill **Finding Messages**

Concept

Occasionally you will want to find an e-mail concerning a project or a business idea, but you will not be able to remember which e-mail it is, based on the subject line and the sender. To aid you in your search, Microsoft has equipped Outlook 2000 with an Advanced Find feature. Mastering this feature will enable you to locate those "lost" e-mails.

Do It!

Virginia will use the Advanced Find feature to locate an e-mail.

1. The VReynolds Practice Inbox must be open to do this exercise.

2. On the Standard toolbar, click the Find button [Find].

3. In the Look for text box of the Find Items in VReynolds Practice Inbox panel, (**Figure 2-18**), type Manet.

4. The Search all text in the message check box should NOT be selected for this exercise. Click [Find Now].

5. The message No Items Found will appear. Click the Advanced Find button [Advanced Find...].

6. When the Advanced Find dialog box opens (**Figure 2-19**), make sure the Messages tab is forward, and type Manet in the Search for the word(s) text box.

7. Select Subject field and message body in the In: box by clicking the drop-down arrow [▼].

8. Click [Find Now].

9. The Book Request e-mail from Jo Hausam is listed in the Information viewer. Double-click on it to read it. After reading, close the e-mail.

10. Click [X] to close the Advanced Find dialog box.

11. Close the Find Items panel by clicking on its Close button.

More

The Advanced Find feature of Outlook offers a variety of ways to find items in the Inbox. For example, if you know to whom you sent the e-mail, click the Sent To button [Sent To...] and Outlook will open the Select Names dialog box so that you can pick a name to search. The same is true if you know from whom you received the e-mail. Click the From button [From...] and Select Names dialog box will be opened, allowing you to choose a name to search.

Figure 2-18 Find Items panel

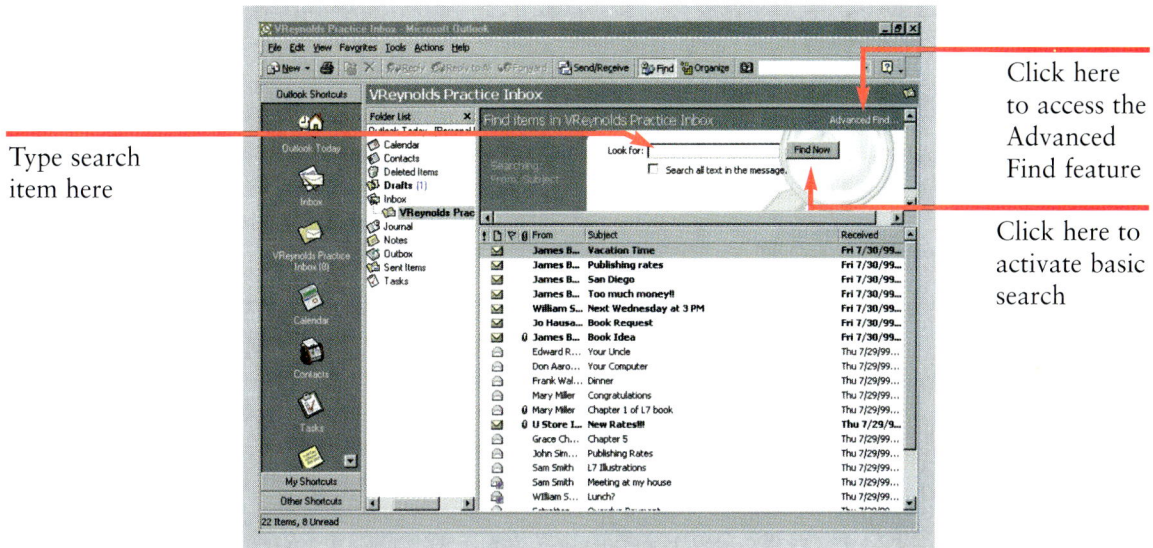

Type search item here

Click here to access the Advanced Find feature

Click here to activate basic search

Figure 2-19 Advanced Find dialog box

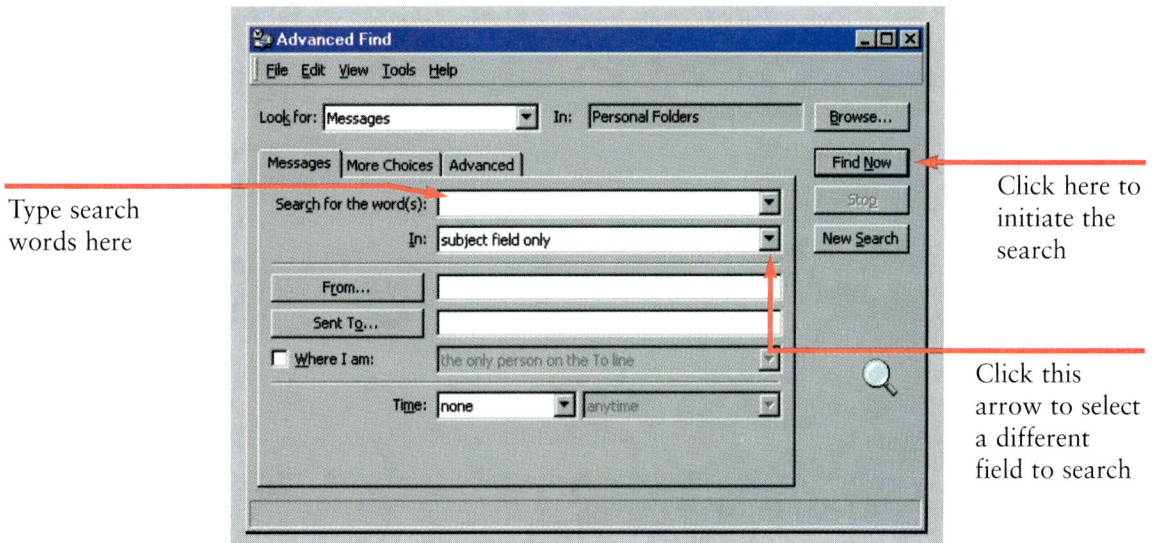

Type search words here

Click here to initiate the search

Click this arrow to select a different field to search

Practice

Open the student practice file, **Prac 2-7** and follow the directions.

Hot Tip

You can access the Find feature quickly by pressing **[Alt]+[I]** on your keyboard.

Using E-Mail Templates

Skill

Concept

Real mail can be sent using a variety of stationery. Outlook 2000 also offers you the option of sending e-mail with different stationery. When sending business e-mail, this option can give your mail a more professional appearance and help it stand out from the other, plain e-mail that is sent.

Do It!

Virginia will select a new stationery to send a congratulatory e-mail to a writer.

1. The VReynolds Practice Inbox must be open to do this exercise.

2. Click the Actions menu to open it. Highlight the New Mail Message Using command. After the submenu opens, click More Stationery.

3. The Select A Stationery dialog box opens (**Figure 2-20**). Click on Ivy. Click [OK] .

4. An untitled Message form opens with the new stationery and Virginia's business signature.

5. Address the e-mail to Bwalters@writer.writer.

6. Type Congratulations as the subject line.

7. In the Message text box, type:
   Bob,
   We are pleased to accept your manuscript for publication. Please contact us regarding payment.

8. Press [Enter] after the last line. Your e-mail should look like **Figure 2-21**.

9. Click [Send] .

More

You can also choose a default stationery which will appear in every e-mail you send. To do so, choose Options from the Tools menu, and click the Mail Format tab. From the Use this stationery by default list, select the design of your choice and click [OK] .

If your recipients do not have an e-mail program that supports HTML formatting they will not be able to see your stationery. You may receive a warning message in the Plain Text Recipient Warning dialog box advising you that some recipients may prefer plain text messages.

To more quickly access the Select a Stationery dialog box you can customize your Menu bar or Standard toolbar to include the More Stationery command. Open the Tools menu and select the Customize command to open the Customize dialog box. Click the Commands tab, select Actions from the Categories scroll box, and click and drag the More Stationery command from the Commands scroll box to the Menu bar.

Figure 2-20 Select a Stationery dialog box

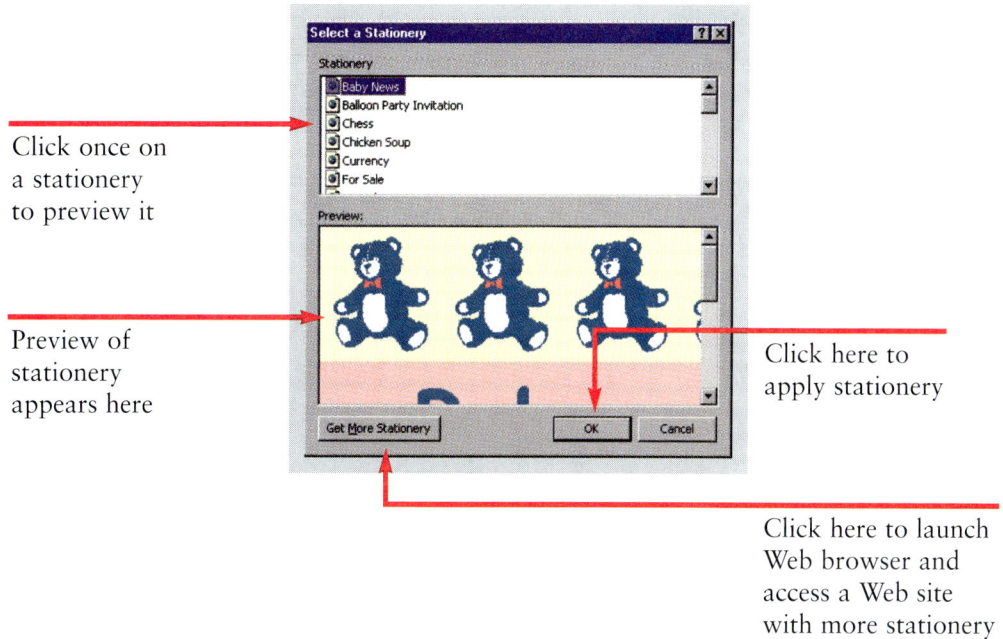

Click once on
a stationery
to preview it

Preview of
stationery
appears here

Click here to
apply stationery

Click here to launch
Web browser and
access a Web site
with more stationery

Figure 2-21 Completed e-mail

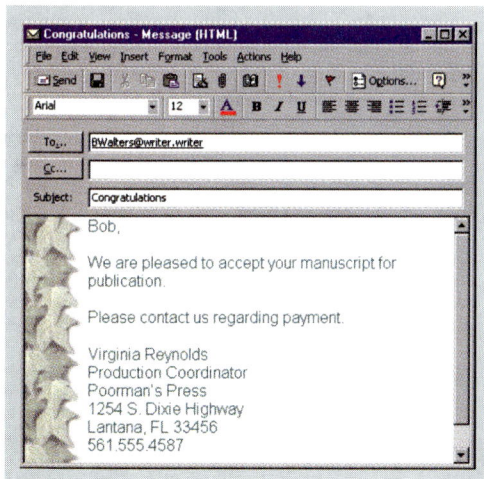

Practice

Open the student practice file, **Prac 2-8**
and follow the directions.

Hot Tip

By clicking the **Get More Stationery** button in the Select a Stationery dialog box, you will connect to the Web, and go to a site which will allow you to download more stationery.

Sorting E-Mail

Concept

Organization is one of the keys to a successful business career. With the wide variety of e-mail that you will receive, it is important to organize mail so that it can be easily located. Simply keeping all messages you have read in your Inbox will lead to a disorderly aggregate of unrelated messages. Outlook 2000 allows you to create folders within the Inbox to sort your mail by subject matter, correspondent, or any category you choose.

Do It!

Virginia will create a folder in her Inbox for e-mail from her supervisor and then transfer the e-mail she has received from him into that folder.

1. The VReynolds Practice Inbox must be open to do this exercise.

2. In the VReynolds Practice Inbox Information viewer, click the Vacation Time e-mail from James Bauler.

3. If the Folder List is not on your screen, click to open the View menu and select Folder List.

4. Click the Organize button [Organize]. Your screen should look like **Figure 2-22**.

5. Click the New Folder button [New Folder...] located in the upper-right corner of the Ways to Organize VReynolds Practice Inbox panel.

6. The Create New Folder dialog box appears (**Figure 2-23**).

7. Be sure that Mail Items is in the Folder contains box. Type Supervisor's Letters in the Name text box. Click [OK].

8. Click [No] when asked if you want to add a shortcut to the Outlook Bar.

9. Click [Create] in the Ways to Organize VReynolds Inbox panel. A message appears stating: This rule will be applied to new messages as they arrive and asking if you would like to run the new rule on the contents of the folder. Click [Yes].

More

Now that you have created the folder and applied the rule to it, all e-mails from James Bauler will automatically be routed into this new folder. By creating other folders and rules, you can set Outlook to sort mail by individuals or companies as it is received.

You can also create rules to automatically empty the Deleted Items folder, forward messages from a particular sender to another person, or delete junk e-mail messages before they ever hit your Inbox.

Finally, you can use a filter to view your Inbox. Open the View menu, highlight Current View, and click Customize Current View. Click the Filter button. From the Filter dialog box, you can choose various options to filter. Once applied, you will only see those e-mails that meet the filter criteria.

Figure 2-22 Organizing the Inbox

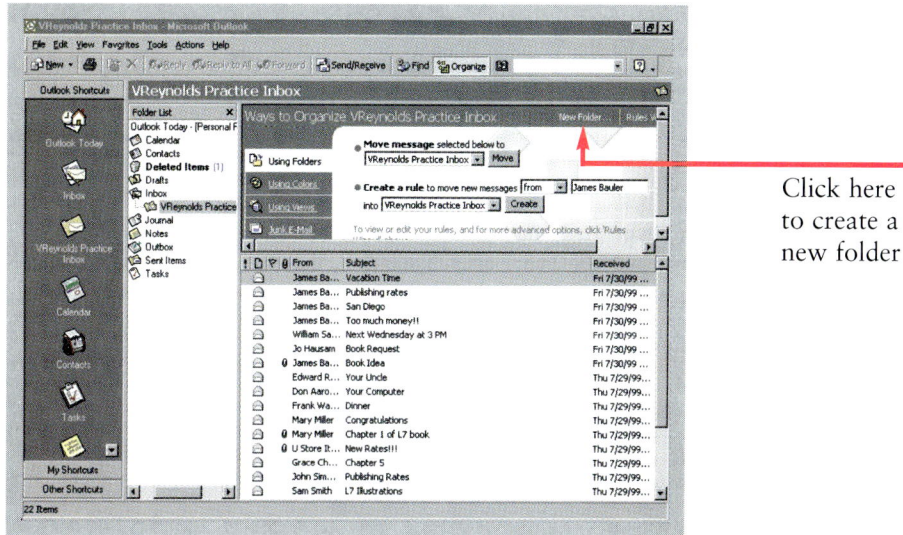

Click here
to create a
new folder

Figure 2-23 Create New Folder dialog box

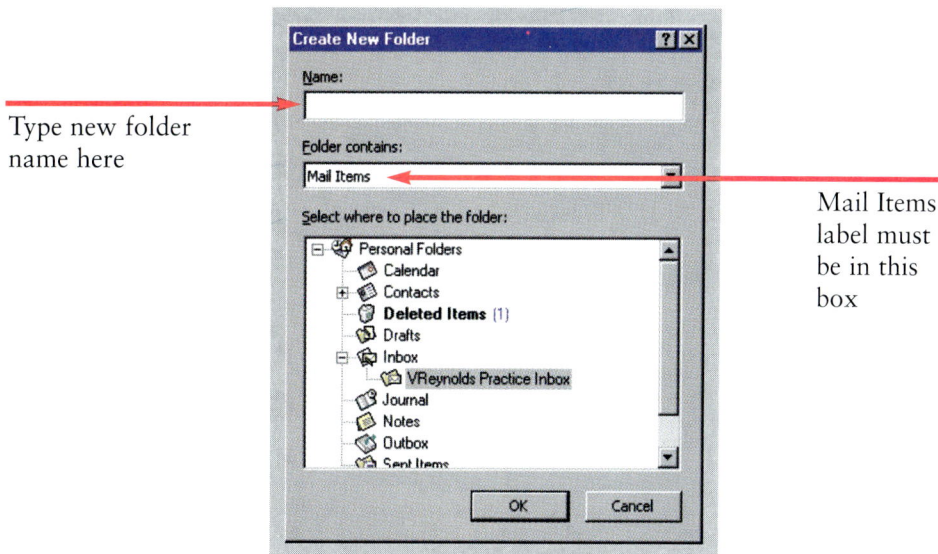

Type new folder
name here

Mail Items
label must
be in this
box

Practice

Create a new folder for **L7 Book Writers** and move all the e-mail from **Mary Miller** into it. Close the Ways to Organize VReynolds Practice Inbox window when you are done.

Hot Tip

To view the contents of a subfolder, click the plus sign **(+)** next to the folder in the Folder List that contains the subfolder you want. Then, click on the subfolder to reveal its contents.

Skill

Setting Viewing Options to Sort E-Mail

Concept

At times, you may receive large amounts of e-mail. Instead of reading each e-mail to find out what it contains, you can customize the view of Outlook so that you can read a short preview of each e-mail. The Preview Pane command can be used to display the complete text of a selected message without having to open it. These features will save you time and effort in your daily work by enabling you to quickly ascertain which messages are imperative or require prompt consideration.

Do It!

Virginia will customize Outlook 2000 to preview each e-mail.

1. You must have the **VReynolds Practice Inbox** open to do this exercise.

2. Open the **View** menu and click **AutoPreview**. The first few lines of each message will be displayed (**Figure 2-24**).

3. Click any message to select it.

4. Open the **View** menu and click **Preview Pane**. The Outlook screen will split into two windows with the previewed messages in the top window and the complete text of the selected message in the bottom window (**Figure 2-25**).

5. Click the **From** column heading in the top pane of the Inbox. The messages are now sorted alphabetically, instead of by date received. Click the **From** column heading again to return the view to normal.

6. Click the **Subject** column heading. The messages are now sorted alphabetically by subject. Click the **Subject** column heading again to return the view to normal.

More

You can rate the level of importance of your messages in the Messages Options dialog box. Double-click an e-mail message in the Inbox to open it. Open the **View** menu and select the **Options** command. In the **Messages** settings section, select **Low**, **Norm** or **High** in the **Importance** list box. Click the **Close** button to save the message. Outlook will prompt you to save the changes. Click **Yes**. Messages you have rated High will be preceded by a ▮. Messages you have rated Low will be preceded by a ↓. Once you have rated your messages, click the ▮ column heading to sort them by order of importance. You can also designate the importance level and the sensitivity level of the messages you send. The sensitivity levels are **Normal**, **Personal**, **Confidential**, and **Private**.

There are other ways to sort your mail using the column headings. The ▮ sorts your mail in order of importance. The ▯ sorts your mail by icon. The ⚑ sorts your mail by flags (flags are used to note messages which require a follow-up action). You can sort your mail by Attachment with the ▯ column heading. Finally, you can sort your mail by the date it was received by clicking on the **Received** column heading.

Figure 2-24 AutoPreview

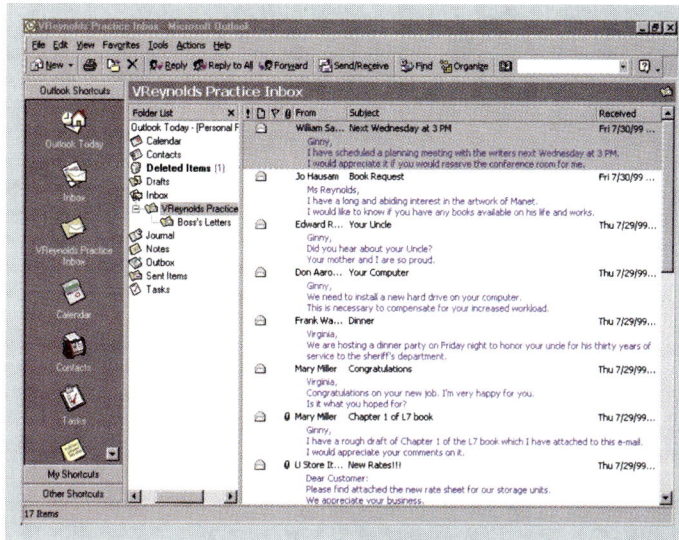

Figure 2-25 AutoPreview and Preview Pane

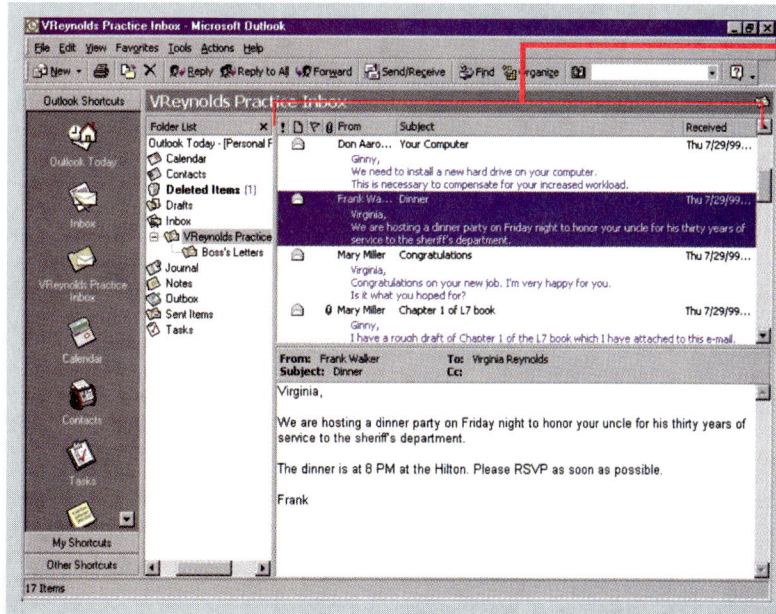

Click these buttons to sort by column heading

Practice

Using the VReynolds Practice Inbox, sort the messages as follows. **(1) List the urgent and private e-mail first. (2) Sort the e-mail alphabetically. (3) Sort so that the "Artist for Hire" e-mail is near the top of the list.**

Hot Tip

You can use these same column headings to quickly organize your **Deleted Items**, **Sent Items**, or **Drafts** folders.

Archiving E-Mail Messages

Concept

Archiving is the method that Outlook uses to store messages that you need to keep, but will probably not reference very often. Archived items are saved on your hard drive in the same folder and subfolders as in Outlook, so that they are easily located for retrieval. Archiving enables you to avoid having to keep these older items on your current screen. Using the AutoArchive feature will keep your screen from becoming cluttered, enabling you to focus on priorities.

Do It!

Virginia will configure Outlook to AutoArchive her messages every other day.

1. The VReynolds Practice Inbox must be open to do this exercise.

2. Open the Tools menu, and click Options.

3. Click the Other tab in the Options dialog box.

4. Click the AutoArchive button [AutoArchive...]. The AutoArchive dialog box will open (**Figure 2-26**).

5. AutoArchive is set to archive every 14 days by default. To change this, click the down arrow next to 14 until it reads 2. Make sure the check box at the beginning of AutoArchive every 2 days is checked.

6. Click the check box to Prompt Before AutoArchive.

7. Click once in the Default Archive File text box to position the insertion point and press the right arrow key until the insertion point is at the beginning of the word Archive in the file string (**Figure 2-27**).

8. Type test. The word archive should now read testarchive.

9. Click [OK] to close the AutoArchive dialog box.

10. Click [OK] to close the Options dialog box.

More

Now that you have set the AutoArchive option, it will prompt you every two days to archive all folders and messages that meet the criteria. This will occur shortly after you launch the Outlook program that day.

Items in any Outlook folder can be archived except the Contacts folder. If you need to reference an archived item, you can import its folder back into Outlook. The default aging periods for Calendar, Tasks, and Inbox are six months. The Deleted Items and Sent Items folders are AutoArchived every two months by default. Auto-Archive can be programmed to create an orderly system for automatically removing expired items from Outlook to suit your particular work environment.

Figure 2-26 AutoArchive dialog box

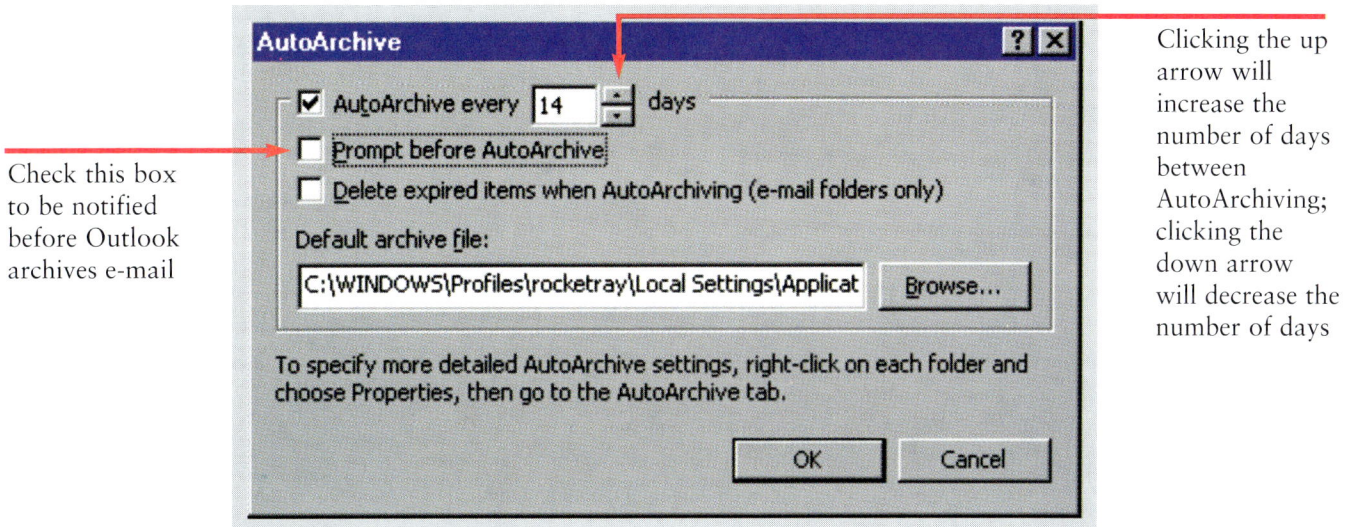

Check this box
to be notified
before Outlook
archives e-mail

Clicking the up
arrow will
increase the
number of days
between
AutoArchiving;
clicking the
down arrow
will decrease the
number of days

Figure 2-27 AutoArchive file string

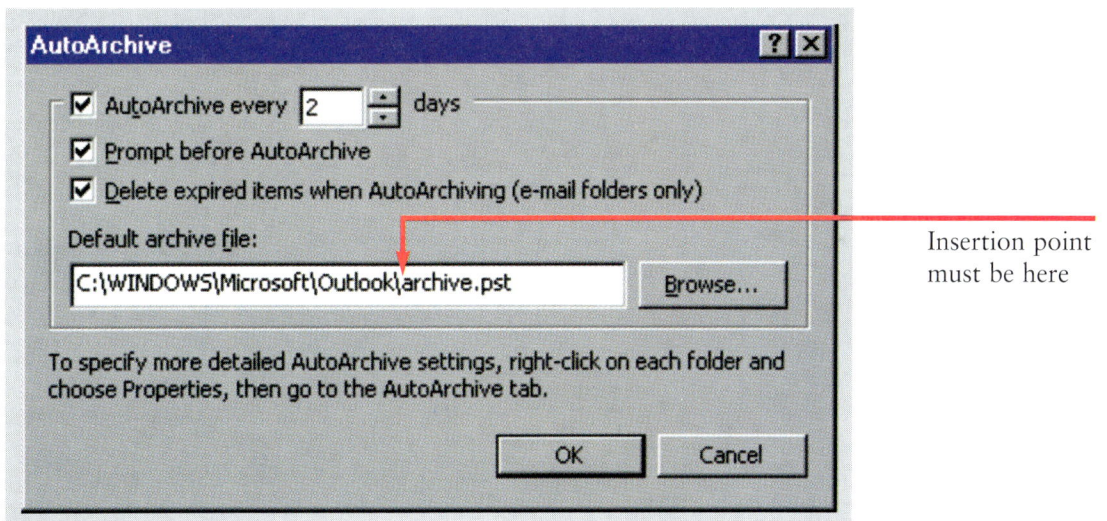

Insertion point
must be here

Practice

Create a new folder in the VReynolds
Practice Inbox titled **Upcoming Projects**
and set Outlook to AutoArchive this folder
every seven days.

Hot Tip

If you do not wish a particular message to
be AutoArchived, open that message, click
the **File** menu and select **Properties**. Click
the **Do Not AutoArchive This Item** checkbox and then click **OK**.

Shortcuts

Function	Button/Mouse	Menu	Keyboard
Save an e-mail	Save	Click File, then click Save	[Ctrl]+[S]
Send an e-mail	Send	Click Tools, then click Send	[Ctrl]+[Enter]
Send/Receive all mail	Send/Receive	Click Tools, then click Send/Receive	
Reply to mail	Reply	Click Actions, then click Reply	[Ctrl]+[R]
Reply to All	Reply to All	Click Actions, then click Reply to All	[Ctrl]+[Shift]+[R]
Forward mail	Forward	Click Actions, then click Forward	[Ctrl]+[F]
Open the Outlook Address Book		Click Tools, then click Address Book	[Ctrl]+[Shift]+[B]
Print any document		Click File, then click Print	[Ctrl]+[P]
Create a new mail message	New	Click Actions, then click New Mail Message	[Ctrl]+[N]
Find an e-mail	Find	Click Tools, then click Find	
Organize the Inbox	Organize	Click Tools, then click Organize	

Quiz

Identify Key Features

Name the items indicated by callouts in **Figure 2-28**.

Figure 2-28 Features of the Inbox and e-mail

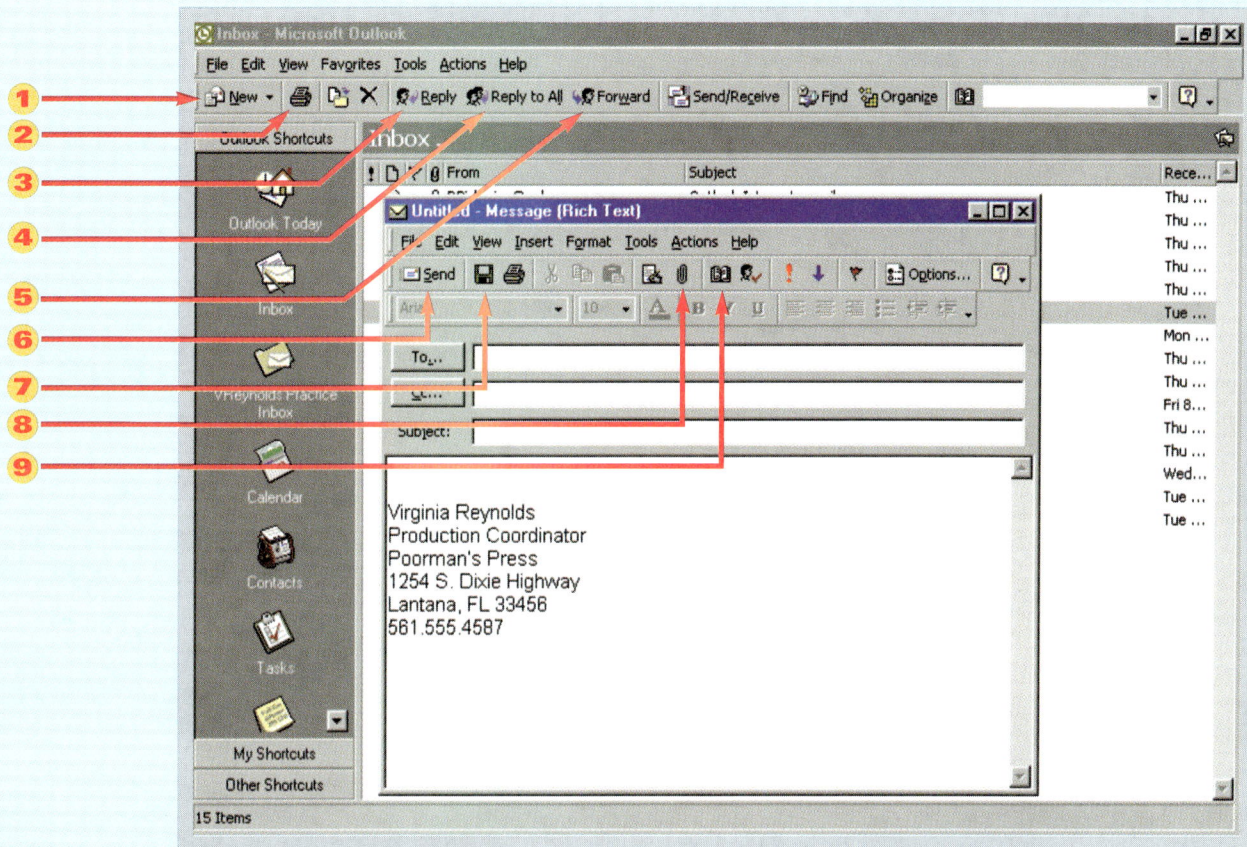

Select The Best Answer

10. Click this to open a blank Message form

11. Stores information about contacts and e-mail addresses

12. Allows you to retrieve an e-mail

13. Will help you locate lost e-mail

14. The background upon which you create an e-mail

15. Allows you to send an e-mail on to a different recipient

16. Indicates that a file has been sent with an e-mail

17. This feature allows you to store e-mail automatically

a. AutoArchive

b. Forward button

c. Outlook Address Book

d. New Mail Message button

e. Template

f. Attachment icon

g. Recall This Message command

h. Find button

Quiz (continued)

Complete the Statement

18. The correct shortcut for opening a new, blank
    Message form is:
    a. [Ctrl]+[B]
    b. [Ctrl]+[N]
    c. [Ctrl]+[Shift]+[N]
    d. [Ctrl]+[E]

19. To create a response to the individual who sent you
    an e-mail, you should click:
    a. The Forward button
    b. The Reply to All button
    c. The Reply button
    d. The Find button

20. To create a response to all the people the e-mail was
    sent to, you should click:
    a. The Forward button
    b. The Reply to All button
    c. The Reply button
    d. The Find button

21. To empty your Inbox of all outgoing e-mail and to
    retrieve all incoming e-mail, click:
    a. The Send button
    b. The Organize button
    c. The Send/Receive button
    d. The Attachment button

22. Pressing [Ctrl]+[Enter] will:
    a. Send the e-mail.
    b. Open a new, blank Message form
    c. Archive the message
    d. Print the e-mail

23. Names, e-mail addresses, and personal information
    are kept in:
    a. The AutoArchive facility
    b. The Calendar
    c. The Outlook Address Book
    d. The Taskpad

24. To locate a lost e-mail, click:
    a. The Organize button
    b. File, then click Help
    c. Actions, then click Retrieve
    d. The Find button

25. The first step towards sorting e-mail is to click:
    a. The Organize button
    b. File, then click Help
    c. Actions, then click Organize
    d. The Find button

26. The view that allows you to see the first few lines of
    each e-mail is called:
    a. Preview Pane
    b. Line view
    c. E-mail view
    d. AutoPreview

Interactivity

Test Your Skills

1. Create an e-mail and send it:

   a. Click the VReynolds Practice Inbox icon.

   b. Click New Mail Message.

   c. Address to **JBauler@boss.boss**.

   d. Type: **Boss, We need to discuss the book project**.

   e. Click Send button.

2. Add an address to the Outlook Address Book:

   a. Open the Address Book.

   b. Click the New Entry button.

   c. Select New Contact from the dialog box.

   d. Type: **Sean M. Domis** and **SDomis@son.son**.

   e. Click the Save and Close button.

3. Forward an e-mail:

   a. Open any e-mail in the VReynolds Practice Inbox.

   b. Click the Forward button.

   c. Address the forwarded e-mail to: **MMiller@artist.artist**.

   d. Add the message: **Mary, Thought you should see this**.

   e. Click Send.

4. Create a folder to sort personal e-mail:

   a. If the Folder List is not visible in the Inbox, click View, then click Folder List.

   b. Click the New Rates e-mail.

   c. Click the Organize button.

   d. Click the New Folder button.

   e. Use **Personal E-mail** as the title of the folder.

   f. Click the Create button.

Interactivity (continued)

Problem Solving

1. You are in charge of the sales department for a small Internet company. Using Outlook, create an e-mail touting your latest Web site. Select an appropriate stationery for the e-mail. Include such information in the e-mail as the location of the Web site, and the average number of hits per day. Address and send the e-mail to at least ten people. (NOTE: You may make up addresses if you prefer.)

2. You have just been promoted to Editorial Assistant at GhostPress, Inc. Ghost Press is located in Dallas, Texas at 342 Sam Houston Boulevard. The zip code is 76854. Your office is in Suite 1225. Your phone number is (861) 555-2323. Create a business signature for your e-mail based on the information above. Create a personal signature for any address in Dallas, Texas.

3. During the course of an average business day as Director of Communications for KCBD Television in Los Angeles, California, you receive an average of five new e-mails with contact e-mail addresses. Create five contacts and add them to your Outlook Address Book.

4. You cannot find two important pieces of e-mail. You know that one of them concerns a miniature model fair. The other e-mail has something to do with a return credit on merchandise. Using the Find feature of Outlook, locate these two e-mails.

L E S S O N

3

MANAGING A CALENDAR

One of the many advantages to using Outlook is that it helps you to manage your time more effectively. Using Outlook, you have at your disposal an easy-to-navigate Calendar with which you can schedule appointments, meetings and events.

The Outlook 2000 calendar also has a reminder feature, which can be programmed to remind you of upcoming commitments anywhere from five minutes to two days before their occurrence. You can also schedule recurring appointments, plan meetings involving others, schedule multi-day events, and save your Calendar as a Web page.

Time is a precious commodity in the workplace. Time management skills can improve your work performance and make your job easier. The Outlook 2000 Calendar will help you to plan your schedule and keep track of your commitments.

Case Study:
In this lesson, Virginia will use the Outlook 2000 Calendar. She will navigate through the Calendar and schedule appointments and recurring appointments. She will set reminders for important appointments and schedule events, multiday events, and meetings. She will invite others to attend meetings and finally, save her Calendar for publication on the World Wide Web.

Skill

Navigating in the Calendar

Concept

When you open the Outlook Calendar there are three separate and distinct areas in the Information viewer: the Appointment Area, the TaskPad, and the Date Navigator. Each part of the Calendar is effectively coordinated to form a cohesive planning tool. Learning to navigate in the Calendar will familiarize you with the program and prepare you to meet all your scheduling needs.

Do It!

Virginia will navigate through the Outlook 2000 Calendar.

1 With Outlook 2000 open, click the Calendar shortcut icon 📇 on the Outlook bar.

2 When the Calendar opens, you will see three separate areas (**Figure 3-1**): the Appointment Area, the TaskPad, and the Date Navigator.

3 Click on the Appointment Area. This area is divided into half-hour time slots and is highlighted from 8 AM to 5 PM, but you can enter appointments for times other than these as well. By clicking the Day, Work Week, Week, or Month buttons on the Calendar Standard toolbar, you can customize the view of the Appointment Area. (You may need to click the More Buttons button to add the Month button to the Standard toolbar.)

4 Click today's date in the Date Navigator in the upper-right corner of the Information viewer. You can navigate to a particular date on this calendar by clicking it. The date listed in the Appointment Area will change accordingly. You can also use the left and right arrow keys on the keyboard to move through the days. The small arrows in the upper corners of the Date Navigator allow you to move a month at a time. When a date is shown in boldface type, there is at least one event scheduled for that day.

5 Click the left scroll arrow of the Date Navigator to go back one month. Click any date. Notice that the Appointment area now shows that date. Click the right scroll arrow to return to the current date.

6 Click on the TaskPad below the Date Navigator. This area gives you a quick overview of the tasks that are currently on your Tasks list for that day. The TaskPad will be discussed in greater detail in Lesson 4.

More

In addition, Outlook offers you a simple option for customizing the Calendar feature. Between each of the elements of the Calendar (Appointment Area, TaskPad, and Date Navigator) there is a slim gray border. When you rest the mouse pointer over these borders, the cursor becomes a double-headed arrow separated by a line. This indicates that you can click and drag the border to expand or contract that area. In this manner, the Date Navigator can be expanded to show up to a full year. Or, the Appointment Area can be expanded to show all the details of any appointments.

Figure 3-1 Parts of the Outlook Calendar

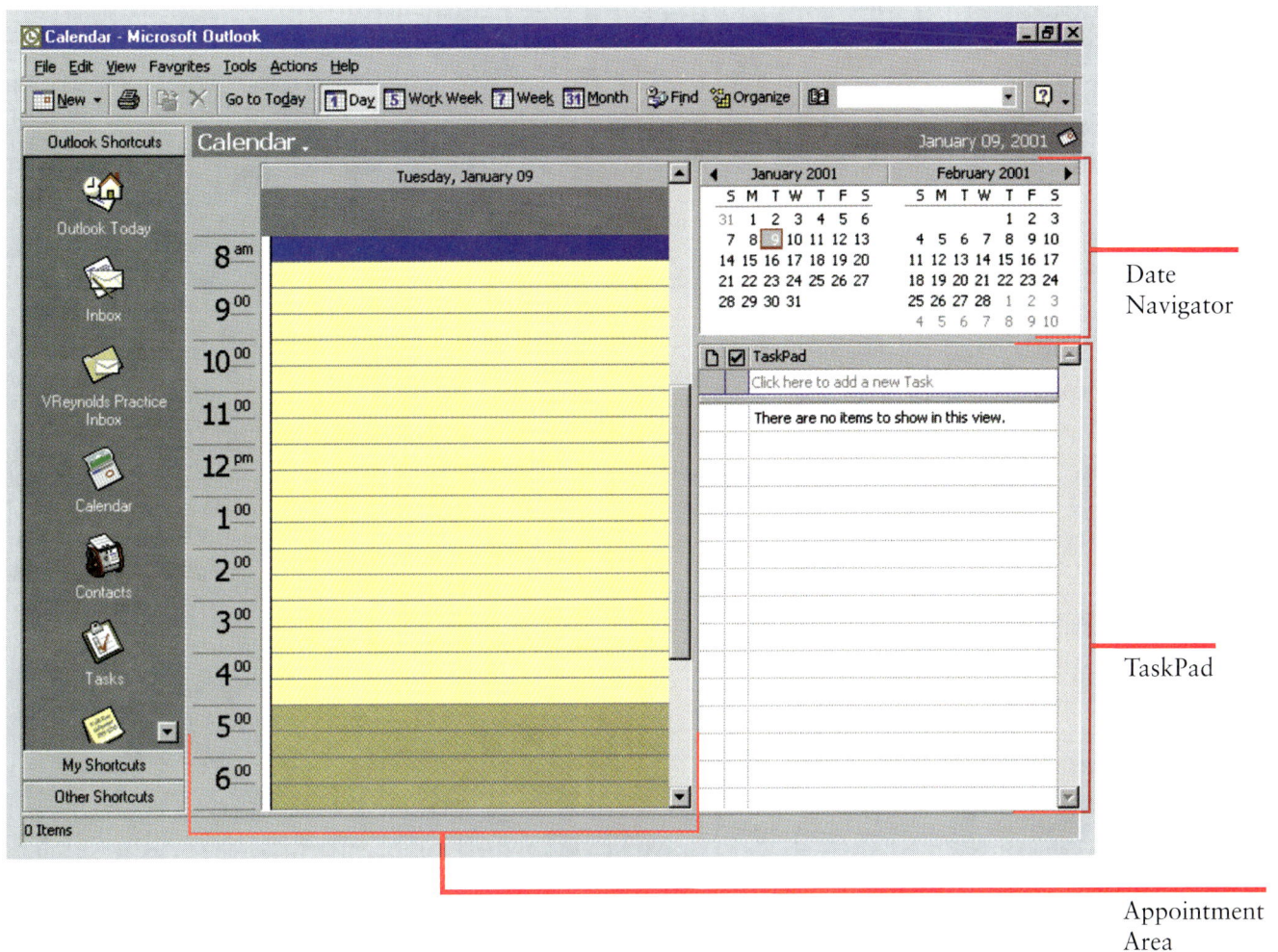

Date Navigator

TaskPad

Appointment Area

Practice

Open the student practice file, **Prac 3-1** and follow the directions.

Hot Tip

To increase the number of months displayed by the Date Navigator, simply click and drag the left border to the left. To decrease the number of months displayed, click and drag the left border to the right.

Skill

Scheduling Appointments and Events

Concept

Scheduling appointments is part of nearly every person's workday. Outlook 2000 allows you to enter your appointment as easily as writing in a date book or a desktop calendar. In addition, there is a feature that helps you schedule all day events.

Do It!

Virginia will schedule a conference with the staff writers for one week from today, and an appointment with her supervisor the day before the conference.

1 If the Calendar is not open, click [icon] on the Outlook Bar.

2 Using the Date Navigator, click the date one week from the current date.

3 Open the Actions menu and click New All Day Event.

4 A blank Event form appears with the default name Untitled (**Figure 3-3**). Type Staff Writers Conference in the Subject text box.

5 Press [Enter]. The event is now scheduled, and there is a gray bar with the conference information at the top of the Appointment Area.

6 Press the left arrow key on the keyboard once to go back one day from the scheduled conference.

7 Click the 12 PM time slot.

8 Type Lunch meeting with boss to discuss conference.

9 Press [Enter]. The meeting is now listed in the Appointment Area (**Figure 3-4**).

More

Outlook also offers an Appointment form for storing more in-depth information about a meeting. To access the form, double-click the appointment in the Appointment Area or right-click the appointment and choose the Open command from the shortcut menu. Now you can designate a place for the meeting and its duration. You can also type a few notes regarding the meeting, and have Outlook send you a reminder.

In the View menu, you can access the Go To Date function (**Figure 3-4**). Alternately, you can access it by pressing [Ctrl]+[G]. This feature allows you to go directly to a specific date by typing the date in the Date text box of the Go To Date dialog box. However, Outlook is programmed to accept ordinary phrases or abbreviations. For example, if today's date is August 5, 2001, and you wish to see your appointments for August 12, 2001, you can type in any one of the following: August 12, 2001, 8/12/01, Aug 12, 2001, or seven days from now.

Figure 3-2 Blank Event form

Type name
of event here

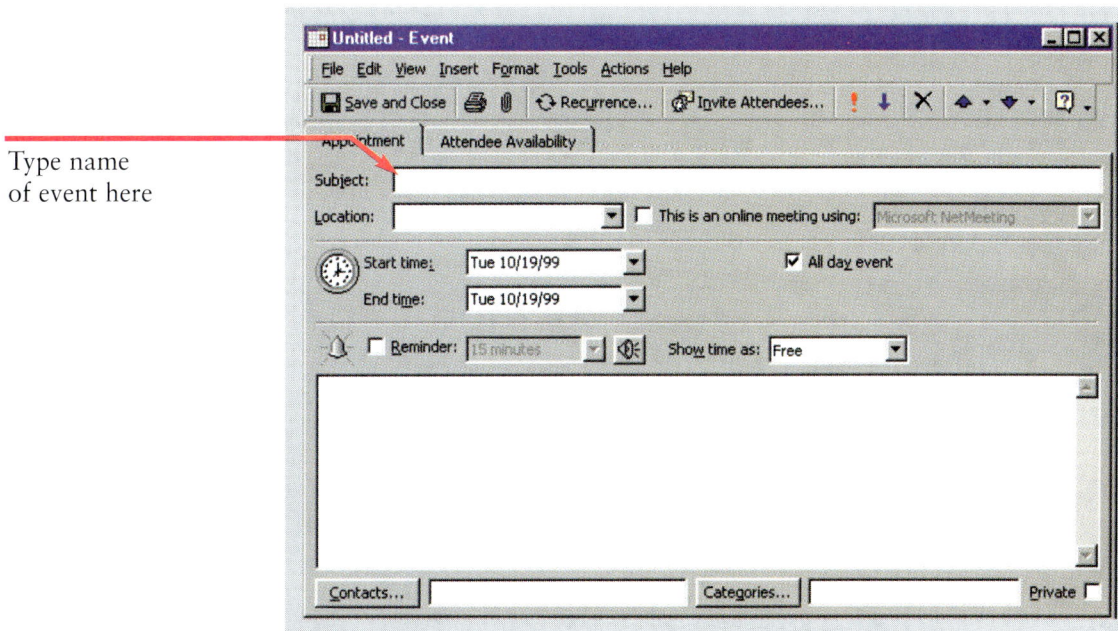

Figure 3-3 Appointment area

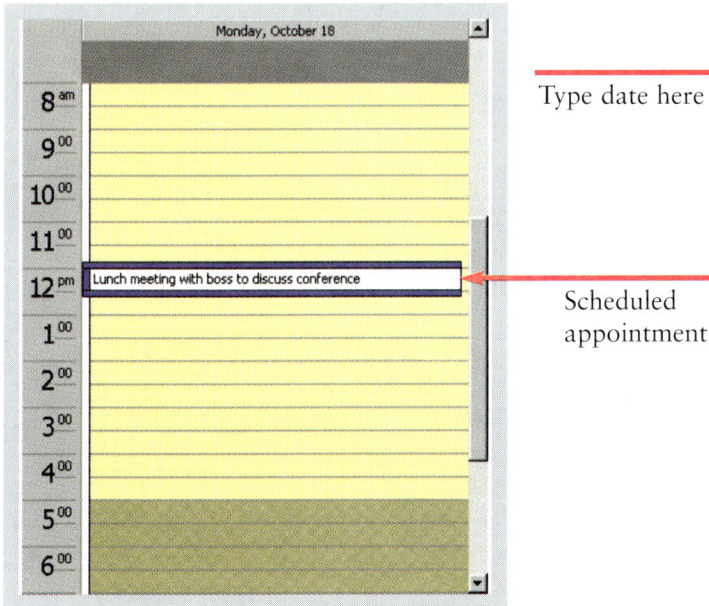

Figure 3-4 Go To Date dialog box

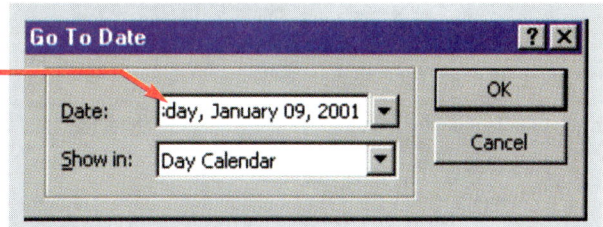

Type date here

Scheduled
appointment

Practice

Open the student practice file, **Prac 3-2** and follow the directions.

Hot Tip

If you must delete an appointment, meeting, or event, use the **Delete** button ☒ on the Standard toolbar. The **[Delete]** key on the keyboard will delete the text only, not the appointment itself.

Skill

Scheduling Multi-day Events

Concept

Work Fairs, Trade Shows, and Expositions are all part of the work world. It is important to be able to schedule large blocks of time to attend or coordinate these events. It is easy to schedule multi-day events using Outlook 2000.

Do It!

Virginia will schedule a weeklong conference for the freelance artists employed by Poorman's Press.

1 Make sure the Calendar is open, with the current date displayed. Click the date **two weeks from the current date** in the Date Navigator.

2 Open the **Actions** menu and click **New All Day Event**.

3 In the blank **Event** form that appears (**Figure 3-5**), type **Freelance Artist Convention** in the **Subject** text box.

4 Type **Conference Room, Boston Office** in the **Location** list box.

5 The **Start Time** list box should show the date you selected in Step 1. If it does not, click the **down arrow** ▼ and select the correct date.

6 Click ▼ in the **End Time** list box and select the date **one week after the beginning of the conference**. *Save and Close*

7 Click the Send/Receive button.

8 Click the **Week** button ⏶ Week on the Calendar Standard toolbar. Notice that the days you have scheduled for the conference are now entered as events in your calendar(**Figure 3-6**). If you need to make other appointments during these days while you are at the conference, simply enter them as you would any other nonrecurring appointments.

More

It is important to know how **Event**, **Appointment**, and **Meeting** are defined in the Outlook 2000 Calendar. An event is an activity that lasts 24 hours or longer. An appointment does not involve inviting other people or reserving office space. A meeting is a gathering of other people you invite and for which you might have to reserve office resources such as a conference room.

When you schedule an appointment, event, or meeting, you can designate your time as **Free**, **Tentative**, **Out of Office**, or **Busy**. Appointments are designated "Busy" by default, so no other meetings may be scheduled during them. Events are automatically designated "Free" so you can schedule other appointments during them.

Figure 3-5 Event form

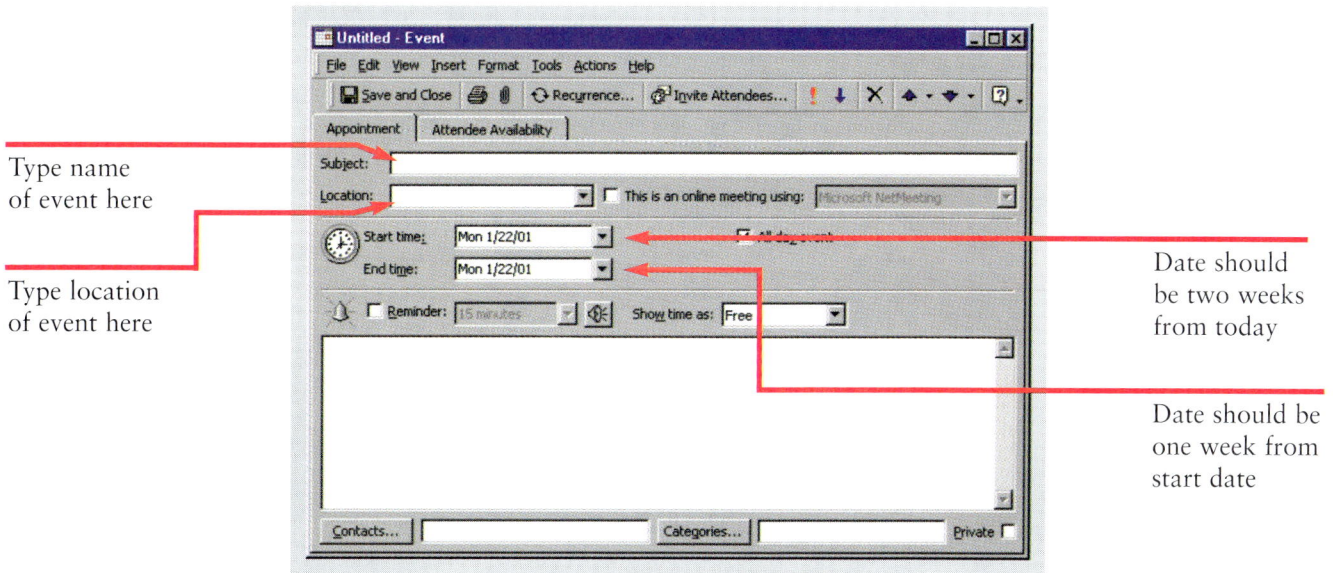

Type name
of event here

Type location
of event here

Date should
be two weeks
from today

Date should be
one week from
start date

Figure 3-6 Scheduled conference

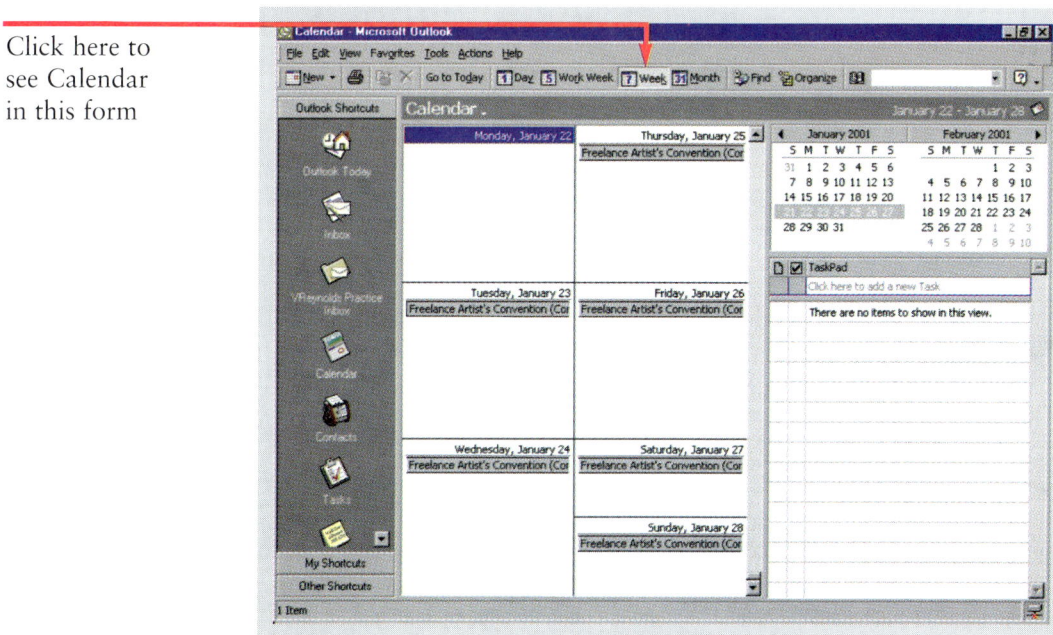

Click here to
see Calendar
in this form

Practice

Open the student practice file, **Prac 3-3** and follow the directions.

Hot Tip

Use the **Show time as** list box in the Appointment, Event or Meeting form to change the status of a commitment from Busy to Free, Tentative or Out of Office.

Skill

Setting Reminders

Concept

You will not want to miss any of your appointments, meetings or events. Outlook 2000 has a reminder system that will automatically alert you to upcoming commitments as far ahead of time as you choose.

Do It!

Virginia will set a reminder for her appointment with her boss.

1 Make sure the Calendar section of Outlook is open with the current date displayed.

2 Select the date two weeks from today in the Date Navigator.

3 Click the 10 AM time slot in the Appointment Area and type: Meeting with Boss to discuss raise. Press [Enter].

4 Double-click the Meeting with Boss appointment you just entered.

5 When the Appointment form appears, (**Figure 3-7**) make sure the Reminder check box is selected. If it is not, click to select it.

6 Click ▼ in the Reminder list box.

7 Select 30 minutes to have Outlook display a pop-up Reminder Notice 30 minutes prior to the scheduled meeting.

8 Click the 🖫 Save and Close button on the Appointment form. After the form closes, a small alarm icon will be displayed in front of the scheduled meeting to indicate that a reminder has been set (**Figure 3-8**).

More

There are three things you can do to a Reminder Notice once it appears on your screen:

1. Click ⬚ Open Item ⬚ to access the Appointment form and review it.

2. Click ⬚ Dismiss ⬚ to close the Reminder and not be reminded again.

3. Click ⬚ Snooze ⬚ to be reminded again. (When you click Snooze, the Reminder will recur in five minutes by default. If you wish to change the amount of time to snooze, click the drop-down arrow at the bottom of the Reminder box.)

You can set a default reminder time for all new appointments rather than setting them on an individual basis. Open the Tools menu and select the Options command. Click the Preferences tab in the Options dialog box. In the Calendar section, select the Default reminder check box. Select a time in the Default reminder list box and click ⬚ OK ⬚ .

Figure 3-7 Appointment form

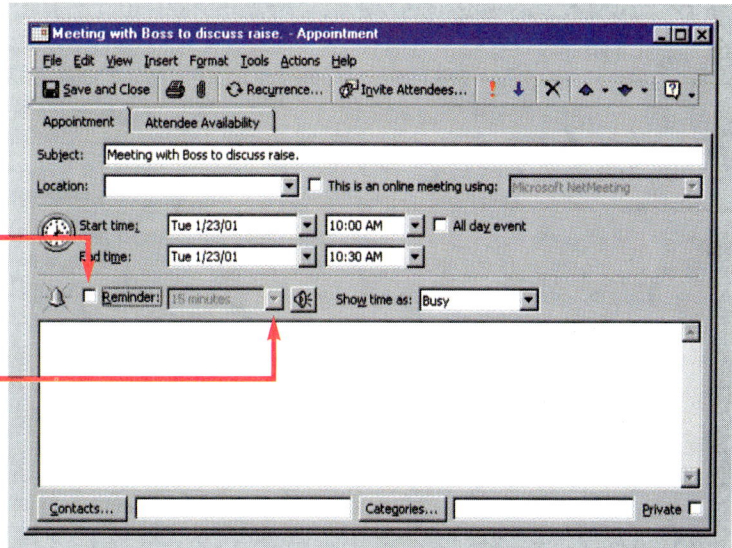

Click here to set a
reminder for this
meeting

Click here to
change time of
reminder

Figure 3-8 Reminder icon

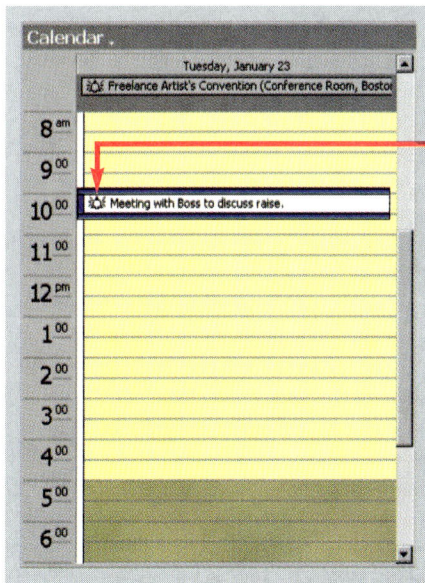

Icon indicates
a reminder has
been set for
this meeting

Practice

Open the student practice file, **Prac 3-4**
and follow the directions.

Hot Tip

If you do not want to be reminded of items
in your Calendar, clear the Default reminder
checkbox.

Skill

Scheduling Recurring Appointments

Concept

Certain appointments occur at regular intervals, for example, a weekly staff meeting. Instead of entering each staff meeting one at a time or copying it from one week to the next, you can program Outlook to schedule a recurring appointment.

Do It!

Virginia's supervisor has asked her to attend a monthly editor's planning session the first Wednesday of every month at 3 PM. Virginia will use Outlook to schedule this recurring appointment.

1. Make sure the Calendar section of Outlook is open with the current date displayed.

2. Click the first Wednesday of next month in the Date Navigator.

3. Click the 3 PM time slot and type: Editor's Planning Session. Press [Enter].

4. Double-click the appointment to access the Appointment form.

5. Click the Recurrence button [⟳ Recurrence...] on the Appointment form's Standard toolbar.

6. The Appointment Recurrence dialog box opens (**Figure 3-9**). In the Recurrence pattern section, select the Monthly radio button.

7. Click the Wednesday radio button to designate that the meeting will reoccur on the first Wednesday of every month. This is the appointment's Range of recurrence.

8. Click [OK] to close the Appointment Recurrence dialog box.

9. Click [💾 Save and Close] on the Appointment form's Standard toolbar.

10. The Appointment now appears with the Recurrence icon in front of it (**Figure 3-10**). This indicates that another appointment is set one month from this appointment.

More

To change a one-time appointment into a recurring appointment, double-click the appointment you wish to change and click [⟳ Recurrence...] on the Appointment Standard toolbar. Set the Recurrence pattern and Range of recurrence in the Appointment Recurrence dialog box.

You can also change one appointment in a series of recurring appointments. Double-click the appointment to access the Open Recurring Item dialog box. Click the Open this occurrence radio button.

You can customize your Menu bar to include the New Recurring Appointment button. Open the Tools menu and select the Customize command to open the Customize dialog box. Click the Commands tab, select Actions from the Categories scroll box and click and drag the New Recurring Appointment command from the Commands scroll box to the Menu bar.

Figure 3-9 Appointment Recurrence dialog box

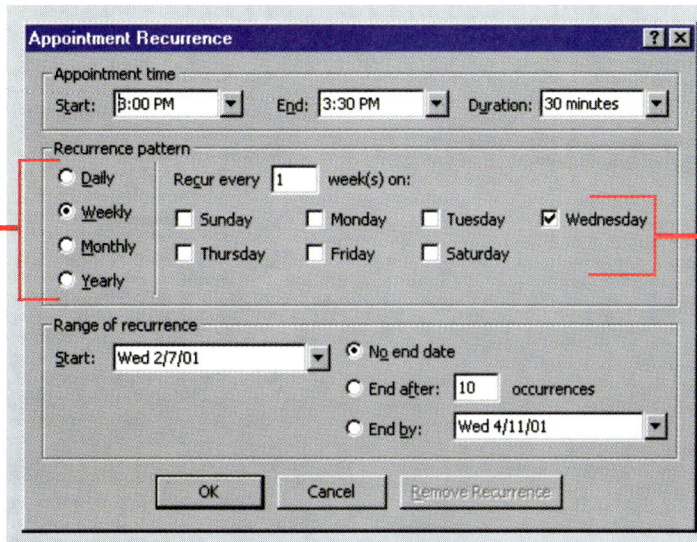

Click here to
set recurrence
pattern

Click here to
select a day for
the recurrence
to occur

Figure 3-10 Recurrence icon

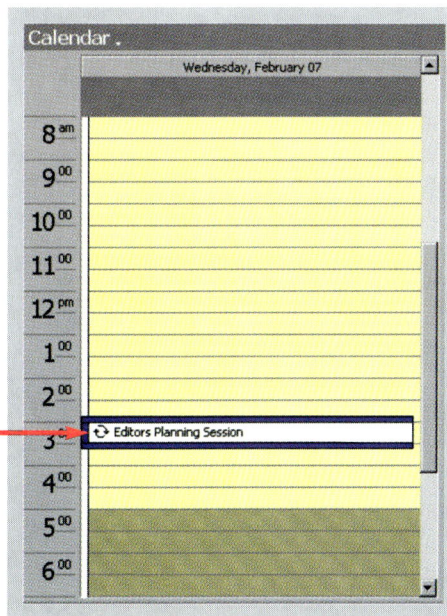

This icon
indicates
that this is a
recurring
appointment

Practice

Open the student practice file, **Prac 3-5**
and follow the directions.

Hot Tip

To change the time or location of all the
recurring meetings in a series, click the
Open the Series radio button.

Skill

Planning Meetings Involving Others

Concept

Meetings are an integral part of the daily business regimen. At some point, you will be called upon to either attend or plan a meeting. Using Outlook 2000, you can set a location, reserve office resources such as projection equipment and use e-mail to invite participants.

Do It!

Virginia has been instructed to plan a meeting involving the writers and artists this coming Monday at 2 PM.

1. Make sure the Calendar section of Outlook is open with the current date displayed.

2. Open the Actions menu and select the Plan a Meeting command. The Plan a Meeting dialog box will open (**Figure 3-11**).

3. Click the `Invite Others...` button. The Select Attendees and Resources dialog box opens with the practice contacts listed (**Figure 3-12**).

4. Click the first contact, and then click the `Required ->` button. The first contact is added to the meeting.

5. Using the same procedure, add the other names to the Required scroll box.

6. Click `OK`.

7. Using the horizontal scroll bar on the scheduling calendar in the Plan a Meeting dialog box, scroll until you view next Monday.

Figure 3-11 Plan a Meeting dialog box

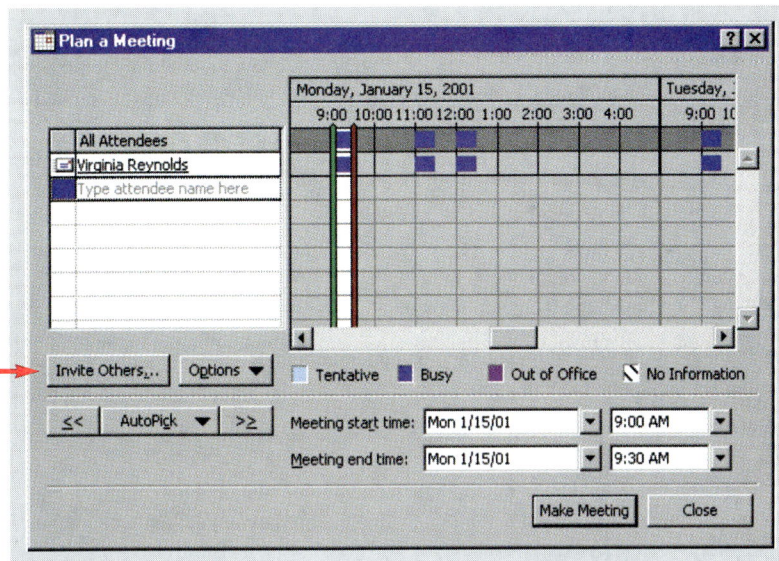

Click here to access the Select Attendees and Resources dialog box

Figure 3-12 Select Attendees and Resources dialog box

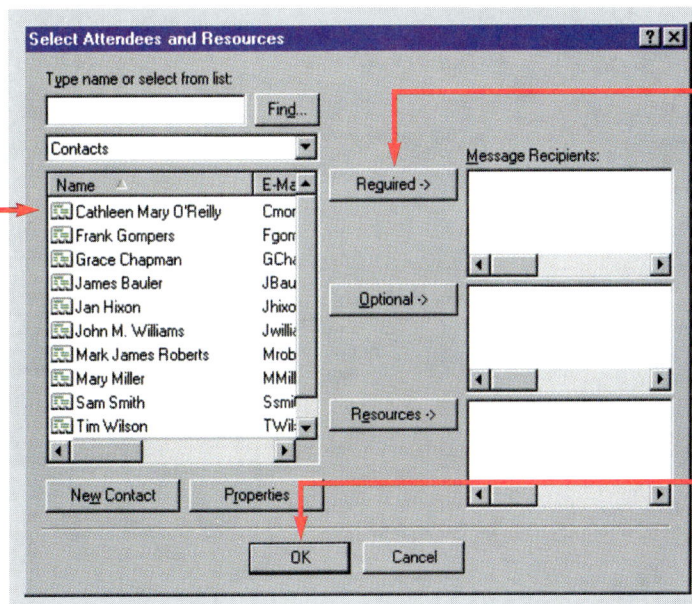

Click here to add selected name to required list

Click here to select name

Click here when finished

Skill

Planning Meetings Involving Others (continued)

Do It!

8 Click once in the gray area directly below the 00 in 2:00 PM. A vertical white bar will appear indicating the time the meeting is now scheduled (**Figure 3-13**).

9 Click the Make Meeting button at the bottom of the Plan a Meeting dialog box. An blank Meeting form appears listing all those invited to the meeting in the To: text box (**Figure 3-14**).

10 Type Mandatory Meeting in the subject line.

11 Click Send on the Meeting form.

12 Click X in the Plan a Meeting dialog box.

More

If you are using Outlook in a Corporate/Workgroup environment, your network administrator will add the names of common resources such as conference rooms and projectors to your company contact list. Scroll through the list, select the appropriate resource, and "invite" it by clicking the Resources -> button.

When you plan a meeting you can designate whether a participant is required to attend or whether attendance is optional. The AutoPick ▼ button in the Plan a Meeting dialog box will direct Outlook to check the schedules of all attendees in your workgroup and choose a time when everyone is free. This option is available when using Outlook in a Corporate/Workgroup environment where everyone is connected on a LAN (Local Area Network).

On the Free/Busy bar in the Plan a Meeting dialog box, light blue will indicate that an attendee is tentatively free. Dark blue indicates that an attendee is busy and purple indicates that an attendee is presently scheduled to be out of the office. To view the Free/Busy bar after the attendees have responded to the meeting request, open the Meeting form and select the Attendee Availability tab. Click the Show attendee availability radio button. To quickly see details about an attendee's schedule, right-click the Free/Busy bar in the time grid. To see a list of the participants' responses, click the Show attendee status radio button.

If you make a mistake and require the wrong person to attend a meeting, it's quite simple to correct. Double-click to open the meeting in your Calendar. Open the Actions menu. Click the Add or Remove Attendees command to open the Select Attendees and Resources dialog box. Click the name of the person whose attendance is not required to highlight it. Press the [Delete] key on the keyboard to remove the person's name from the Required box.

You can also program Outlook to automatically handle meeting requests that you receive. Click Tools and select Options. Click the Preferences tab, the Calendar Options button, then the Resource Scheduling button. In the Resource Scheduling dialog box, select the Automatically accept meeting requests and process cancellations and the Automatically decline conflicting meeting requests checkboxes, then click OK to close each of the open dialog boxes.

Figure 3-13 Plan a Meeting dialog box

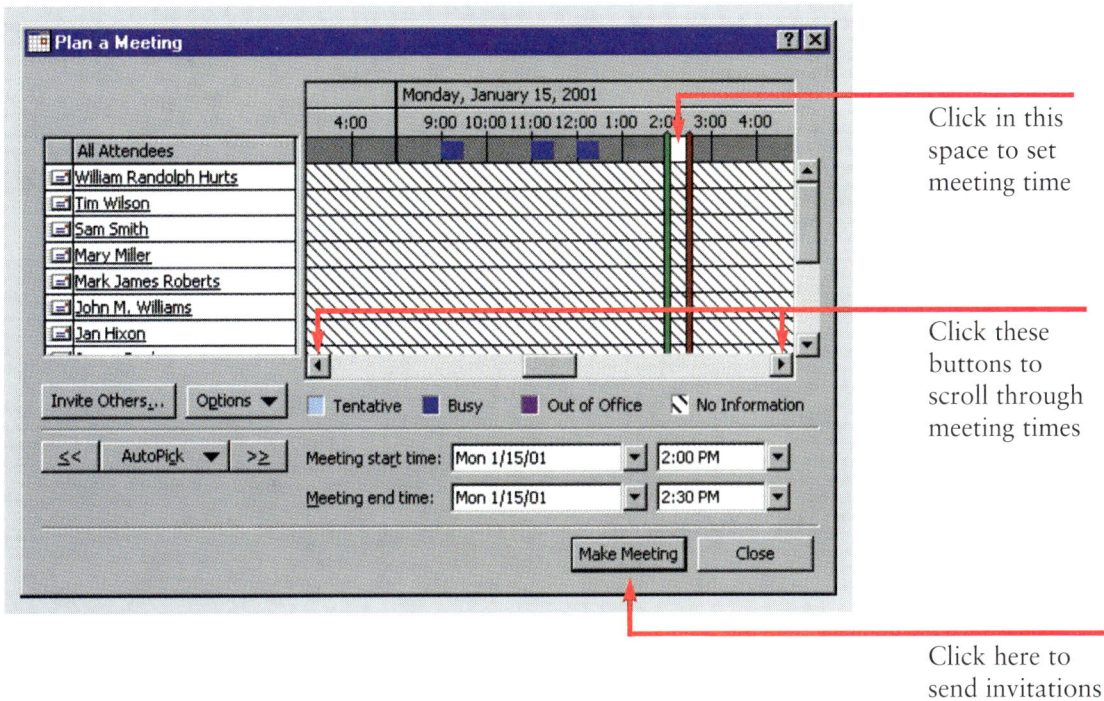

Click in this space to set meeting time

Click these buttons to scroll through meeting times

Click here to send invitations

Figure 3-14 E-mail form

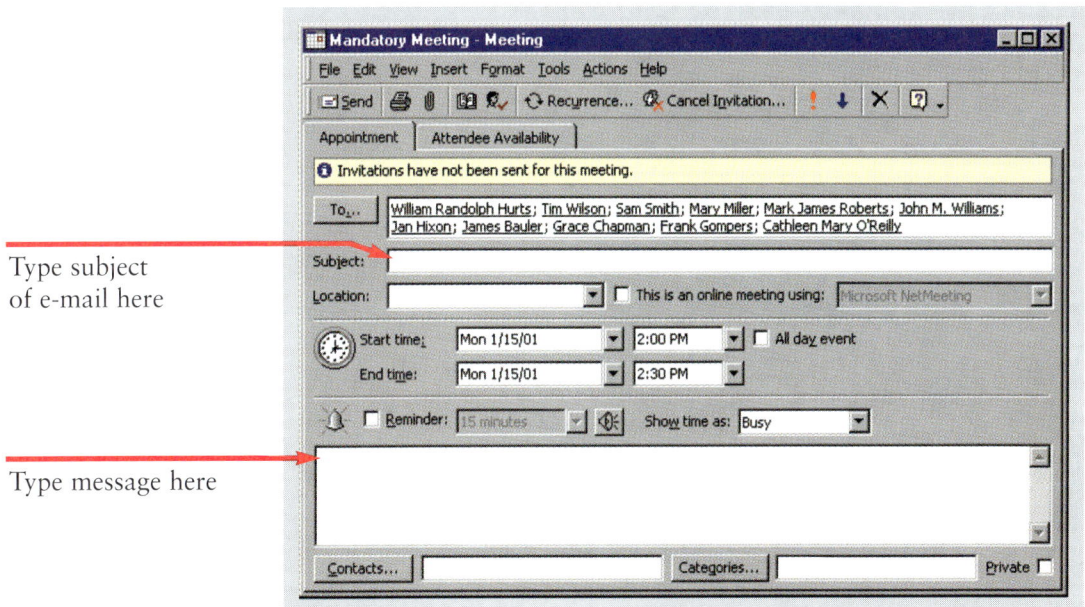

Type subject of e-mail here

Type message here

Practice

Open the student practice file, **Prac 3.6** and follow the directions.

Hot Tip

If you program Outlook to handle your incoming meeting requests, meetings that fit your schedule will be automatically added to your Calendar, and those that do not will be declined. An e-mail about each meeting will be placed in your Inbox.

Skill

Saving a Calendar as a Web Page

Concept

At times you will need to plan meetings or schedule appointments with people outside your office. You can post your Calendar on the World Wide Web so that clients or customers can access it. The Save as Web Page command enables you to save your Calendar in HTML format for publishing on your corporate or personal Web site.

Do It!

Virginia will save a section of her Calendar in HTML format.

1 Make sure the Calendar is open with the current date displayed.

2 If the Folder List is not displayed, open the View menu and select the Folder List command. Your screen should look similar to **Figure 3-15**.

3 Click once on the Calendar in the Folder List.

4 Click File on the Menu bar. Click the Save as Web Page command. The Save as Web Page dialog box appears (**Figure 3-16**).

5 In the Duration area, use the ▼ in the Start and End date list boxes to select the week of the Freelance Artist Convention.

6 In the Save as area, type VReynolds Calendar in the Calendar title text box.

7 In the File name text box, type: VReynolds Calendar.

8 Click the Save button. (NOTE: If the Save as Web Page feature is not installed, you will be prompted to install it.)

More

The Calendar duration you wish to save as an HTML document is not limited. You can publish one day to the WWW, or your Calendar for the next ten years. In the Options section of the Save as Web Page dialog box, you can choose to include appointment details or give your Calendar a background image. You can also open the saved Web page in your browser by selecting the appropriate check box.

If you are using Outlook in the Corporate/Workgroup configuration, you will have to set up a personal Internet account in addition to your corporate Internet account in order to publish your Calendar as a Web page. To do so, open the Tools menu and select the Services command. On the Services tab, select Internet E-mail and click the Add button. On the Add to Services Profile dialog box, select Internet E-mail again and click the OK button. Select the General tab of the Mail Account Properties dialog box, and fill in the information requested, then select the Connect using my phone line radio button. In the Modem section, select the dial up networking connection created for your ISP (Internet Service Provider) from the list box.

Figure 3-15 Calendar with Folder List

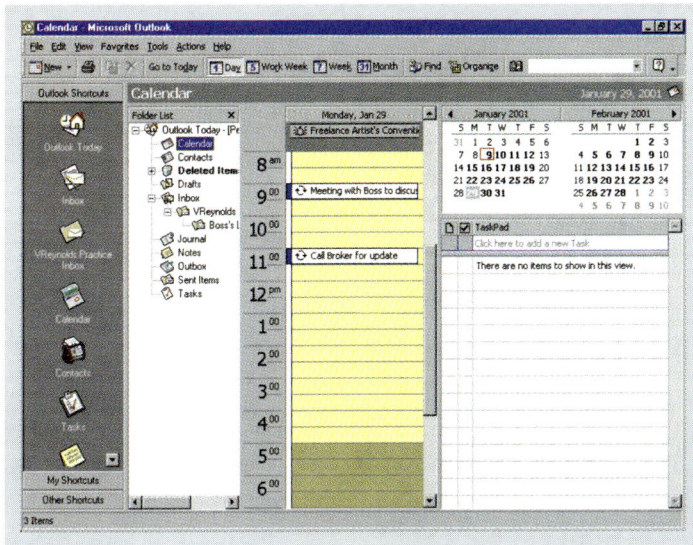

Figure 3-16 Save as Web Page dialog box

Click here to select
duration dates

Change Calendar
title here

Type File
name here

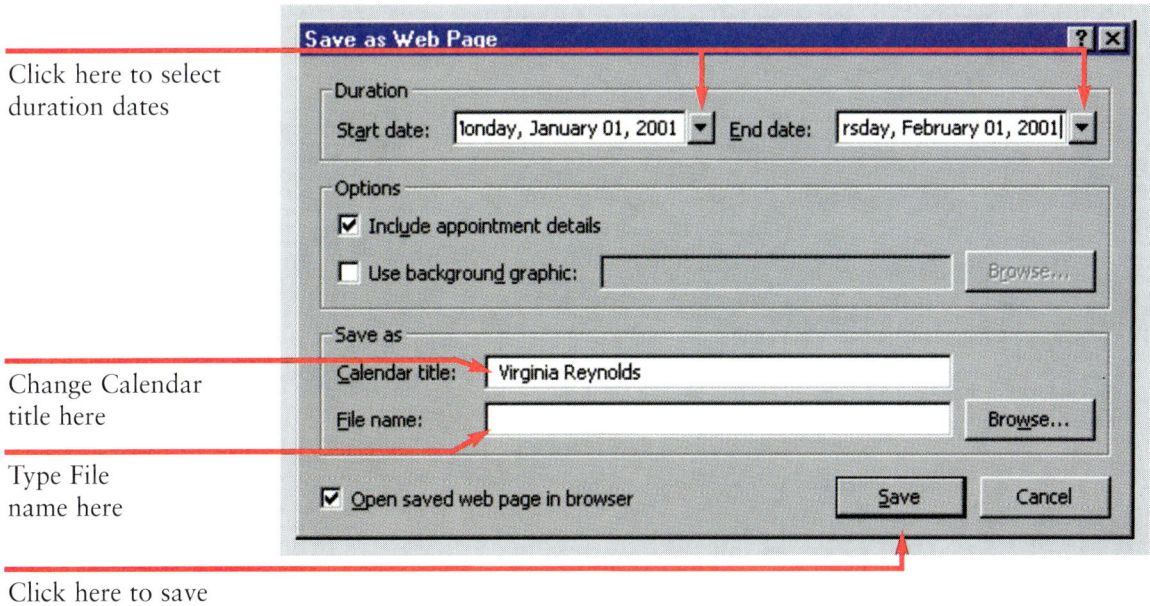

Click here to save

Practice

Open the student practice file, **Prac 3.7** and follow the directions.

Hot Tip

Be aware that whatever you put on the World Wide Web can be viewed by almost anyone. It would be wise not to put too much personal information in a Calendar posted to the Web.

Skill Printing in Calendar

Concept

Because you will have many things to do during a business day, you may not always be at your computer. Nonetheless, you still must keep careful track of your daily appointments. This can be accomplished by printing your daily schedule.

Do It!

Virginia will choose a date and print the schedule for that day.

1 Make sure that the Calendar is open and that any printer connected to your computer is on and working properly.

2 Open the View menu, select Go To, and click Go to Date. The Go To Date dialog box will open.

3 Click the ▼ in the Date list box and select January 16, 2001.

4 Click OK. The schedule for that day will appear in the Appointment area.

5 Click the Print button 🖨 on the Standard toolbar. The Print dialog box will open (**Figure 3-17**) with the Daily Style selected by default.

6 Click Page Setup... . The Page Setup: Daily Style dialog box appears (**Figure 3-18**).

7 Click ▼ in the Layout list box and select 2 pages/day. Click OK.

8 Click OK in the Print dialog box. The printer will now print the schedule for January 16, 2001 in 2 Pages per Day, Daily Style.

More

One of the many uses of the Calendar is its ability to create appointments from e-mails. For example, you might receive an e-mail from an individual requesting a meeting on Tuesday at 4 PM. Instead of accessing a new Appointment form, close the letter, go to the Inbox, and make sure the Folder List is enabled. Now, click and drag the e-mail requesting the appointment from the Inbox to the Calendar folder in the Folder List.

An Appointment form will appear with some of the information already filled in. At this point, simply type in any other information you feel is pertinent to the meeting and click 💾 Save and Close and the meeting will be added to your Calendar.

To print selected days in your Calendar, press the [Ctrl] key and click the days you want to include in the Date Navigator. If the days are consecutive, click and drag to highlight them. You can use the Print Preview command on the File menu to preview the Calendar before you print it. The Print Preview button is also located on the Advanced toolbar. To add the Advanced toolbar to your screen, open the Tools menu, highlight Toolbars, and click Advanced.

Figure 3-17 Print dialog box

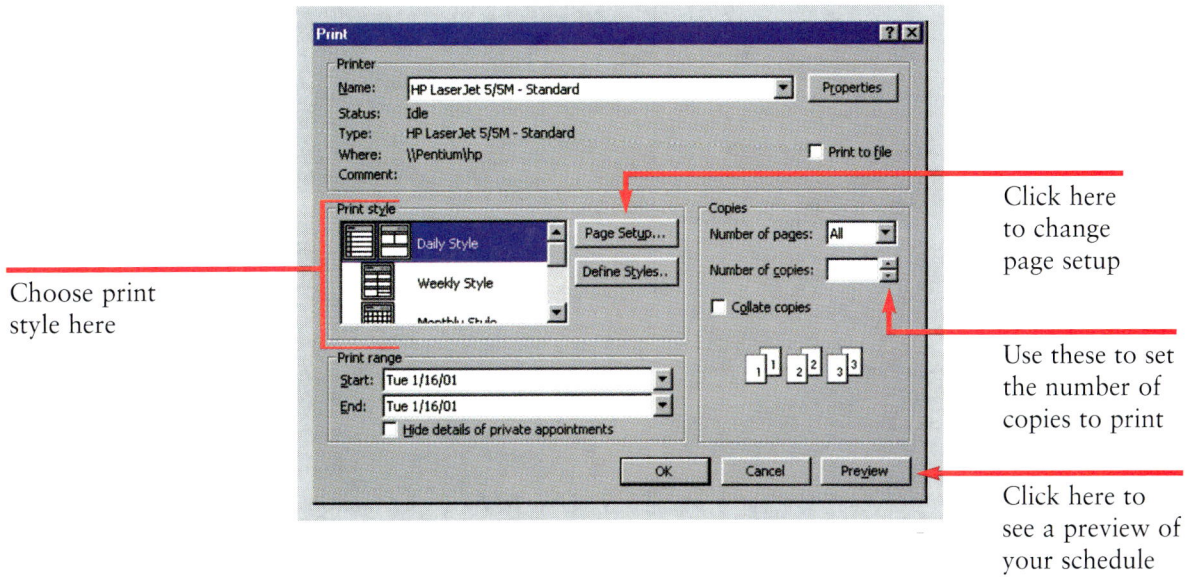

Choose print style here

Click here to change page setup

Use these to set the number of copies to print

Click here to see a preview of your schedule

Figure 3-18 Page Setup dialog box

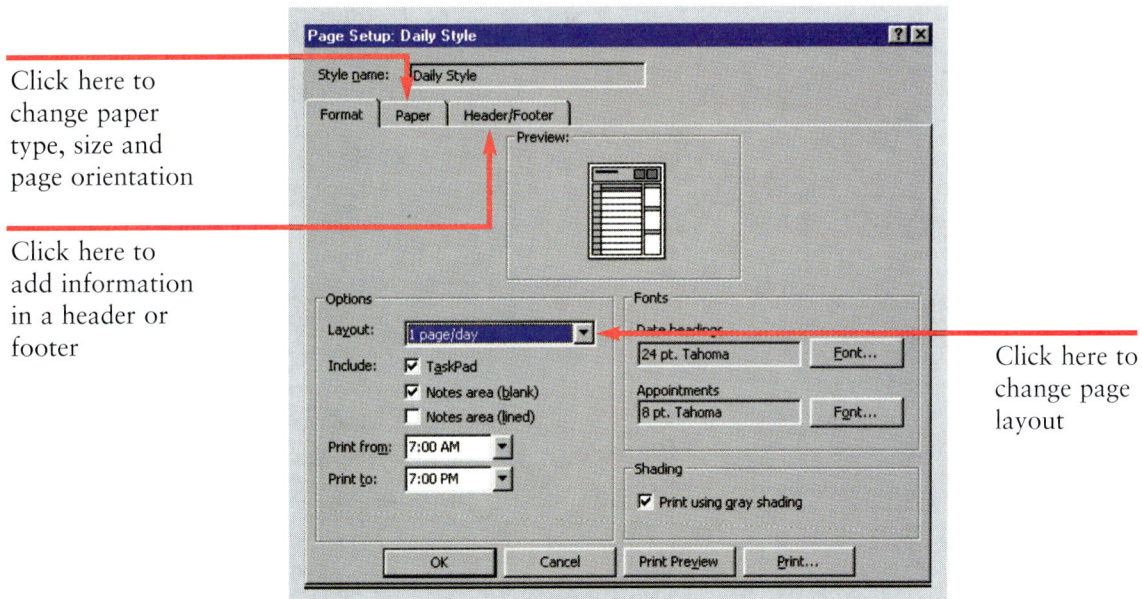

Click here to change paper type, size and page orientation

Click here to add information in a header or footer

Click here to change page layout

Practice

Open the student practice file, **Prac 3.8** and follow the directions.

Hot Tip

Pressing **[Ctrl]+[G]** will take you directly to the Go To Date dialog box.

Shortcuts

Function	Button/Mouse	Menu	Keyboard
Open Calendar		Click View, select Go To, then click Calendar	
Open New Appointment form	New ▾	Click File, then click New Appointment	[Ctrl]+[N]
Save and Close form	Save and Close		[Alt]+[S]
View 1 Day of Calendar	1 Day	Click View, then click 1 Day	[Alt]+[Y]
View 5 Day Work Week of Calendar	5 Work Week	Click View, then click 5 Work Week	[Alt]+[R]
View 7 Day Week of Calendar	7 Week	Click View, then click 7 Week	[Alt]+[K]
View 31 Day Month of Calendar	31 Month	Click View, then click 31 Month	[Alt]+[M]
Set appointment to recur	Recurrence...	Click Action, then click Recurrence	[Ctrl]+[G]
Print daily schedule		Click File, then click Print	[Ctrl]+[P]

Quiz

Identify Key Features

Name the items indicated by callouts in Figure 3-19

Figure 3-19 Calendar features

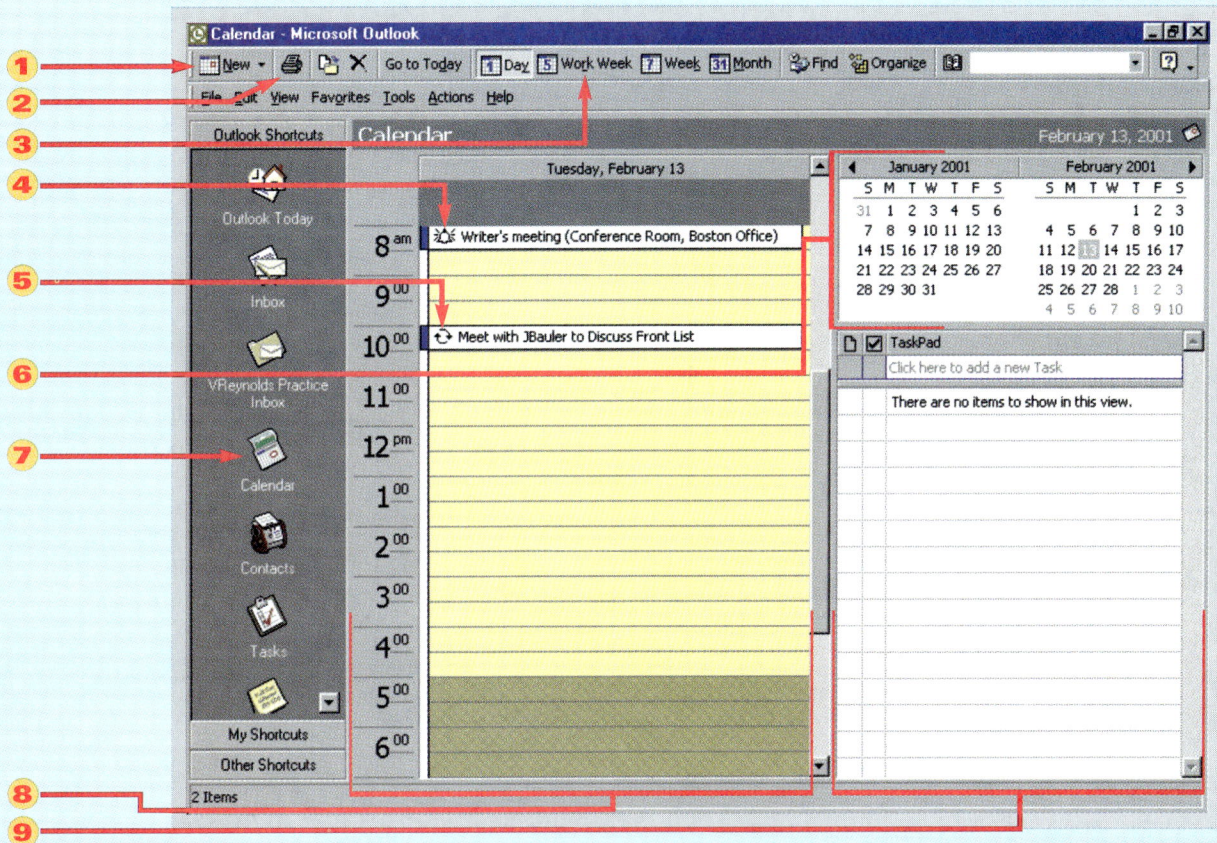

Select The Best Answer

10. Allows you to go directly to the Calendar

11. Allows you to go directly to any day

12. Any activity that lasts 24 hours or longer

13. A gathering of people for business purposes

14. A gathering of two people for business purposes

15. Feature that will inform you of an upcoming activity

16. An activity that occurs at regular intervals

17. The format which allows the saving of a Calendar as a Web page

a. Recurring Appointment

b. Meeting

c. Go To Date function

d. Calendar shortcut icon

e. HTML

f. Reminder

g. Appointment

h. Event

Quiz (continued)

Complete the Statement

18. To activate the Go To Date box, press:
    a. [Ctrl]+[A]
    b. [Ctrl]+[C]
    c. [Ctrl]+[G]
    d. [Alt]+[G]

19. This area of the Calendar lists your daily schedule:
    a. Appointment area
    b. TaskPad
    c. Date Navigator
    d. Standard toolbar

20. If you schedule a business activity for 24 hours or longer, it is called:
    a. A meeting
    b. A symposium
    c. An event
    d. An appointment

21. This is not one of the choices when a Reminder Notice appears on your screen:
    a. Dismiss
    b. Create New
    c. Snooze
    d. Open Item

22. If an appointment or meeting occurs at regular times and intervals, it is said to have:
    a. Occurence
    b. Recurrence
    c. Recuperance
    d. Resurgence

23. The first step to organizing and scheduling a meeting is to click the:
    a. Invite Others command
    b. Select Attendees and Resources button
    c. Required command
    d. Plan a Meeting command

24. The proper command to save your Calendar as a Web page is:
    a. Save as
    b. Save as HTML
    c. Save as Web Page
    d. Save as WWW page

25. This is not one of the options to print your calendar:
    a. Biweekly Style
    b. Daily Style
    c. Monthly Style
    d. Trifold Style

Interactivity

Test Your Skills

1. Schedule an appointment for today at 4 PM:
   a. Double-click the correct time.
   b. Type **Dentist** in the Subject area.
   c. Type **12 Smith Avenue** in the Location area.
   d. Click the Reminder check box.
   e. Click Save and Close.

2. Schedule a recurring appointment for every Monday at 9 AM with the accountant:
   a. Click the first Monday of next week.
   b. Click the 9AM time slot and type Meet with Accountant.
   c. Double-click the appointment.
   d. Click the Recurrence button.
   e. Set the Recurrence pattern for every Monday at weekly intervals.
   f. Save and close the Recurrence and Appointment dialog boxes.

3. Save this week in your Calendar as a Web page:
   a. With Folder List view enabled, click the Calendar and then click File.
   b. Choose the correct command to save the Calendar as a Web page.
   c. Set the duration to save as this business week.
   d. Label the Calendar: **My Calendar**.
   e. Click Save.

4. Print your daily schedule:
   a. Select any day to print.
   b. Click the Print button.
   c. Select Daily Style and click Page Setup.
   d. Select 1 Page/Day as the Layout.
   e. Click Print.

Interactivity (continued)

Problem Solving

1. As Meeting Coordinator for Chemline Industries, you have been instructed to schedule a week-long event. Title the event: **Women in Chemistry**. Schedule it for the second week in February, 2003. Issue an invitation to all the women in your Address Book.

2. You are in charge of the Accounting department. Part of your responsibility is to meet weekly with each department head and monthly with the Board of Directors. There are four departments in the company: Research and Development, New Projects, Payroll, and Human Resources. Schedule recurring appointments for Monday, Tuesday, Wednesday, and Thursday at 9AM for each department, and Monday at 1PM with the Board of Directors.

3. You have been instructed by your boss to plan two meeting involving others. The meetings concern the new stock option plans of the company. Schedule the four hour meetings back-to-back on October 13, 2000. The first meeting starts at 8AM and the second at 1PM. Invite those people with last names beginning with A through K to the first meeting, and those with last names beginning with L through Z to the second meeting.

4. You have been given the following appointments to schedule: 1) April 5, 2001 at 9AM with Sam Johnson to discuss the printing schedule, 2) A meeting each week at 10AM on Monday beginning with the first Monday in April, 2001 with James Bauler to discuss the front list, and 3) A meeting every other Friday, beginning April 20, 2001 at 3PM with Al Simpson of the Human Resources department to discuss new hiring policies.

LESSON 4

MANAGING CONTACTS, TASKS AND NOTES

Throughout this book, we have stressed the virtue of organization. Organization can make the difference between a successful business career and an unsuccessful one. Furthermore, studies have found that organized people experience more enjoyment at work and suffer from less work-related stress. The benefits of organization cannot be emphasized enough. In this chapter, you will learn how to use the Contacts, Tasks, Notes and Journal folders to organize both your business and personal activities.

First you will learn how to store and retrieve a variety of information about the important people in your business or personal life using the Contacts folder. You will learn how to create, edit, and reorganize your contacts in order to quickly and efficiently locate contact information. Then you will learn how to create virtual business cards, which you can attach to outgoing e-mail messages.

Next you will learn how to organize all of your assignments and chores, both business and personal, using the Tasks list. A task may be a meeting you have to attend, a job that requires your ongoing attention, or even a personal task with a specific due date. The Tasks list will enable you to keep track of everything from sales reports and performance reviews to picking up tickets for the ballet and your dry-cleaning.

Then you will learn about electronic notes, which will allow you to eliminate those sticky notes and random pieces of paper that you might normally use to jot down phone numbers, ideas, or insights. You can easily color-code your notes, organize them into categories, or sort them by creation date. You will learn how to use the Outlook Journal. Finally you will learn to integrate Outlook's components to make accomplishing tasks easier and more efficient.

Case Study:
In this lesson, Virginia will create and organize her contacts. Then, she will create tasks, and accept and decline tasks from others. Next, she will create, edit, and customize notes. She will also learn how to create a Journal entry. Finally, she will integrate Outlook's components to accomplish several tasks easily and completely.

Skill

Creating and Deleting Contacts

Concept

Keeping track of all the people you meet in a business environment can prove a daunting task. However, Outlook 2000 provides an effective, easy way to build and maintain a large amount of contacts. Learning to add and delete contacts are the first steps to building a Contacts list.

Do It!

Virginia will add a contact to her Outlook Address Book and delete another contact.

1. Click the Contacts shortcut on the Outlook Bar. The shortcut is indicated by an icon that resembles a Rolodex 📇 .

2. The Contacts Information viewer appears in Address Cards view. Click New Contact ⊡New▾ on the Standard toolbar. A blank Contact form opens with the default name Untitled as shown in **Figure 4-1**.

3. Type Jon Walters in the Full Name text box, and press the [Tab] key once. Notice that the File as list box now reads, Walters, Jon.

4. Type Press Manager in the Job title text box, and press the [Tab] key.

5. Type Royal Printing in the Company text box, and press the [Tab] key three times.

6. Type (561) 555-9898 in the Business text box. Then, press the [Tab] key eight times or click on the Address text box.

7. Type 342 Lantana Road and press the [Enter] key. Type Lantana, FL 33545. Before moving on, make sure the This is the mailing address box is checked.

8. Click the E-mail text box and type Jwalters@royal.press.

9. Click the Categories button at the bottom of the Contact form. The Categories dialog box appears (**Figure 4-2**).

10. Click the check boxes for Business, Holiday Cards, and Supplier.

11. Click ⌷ OK ⌷ to close the Categories dialog box

Figure 4-1 Blank Contact form

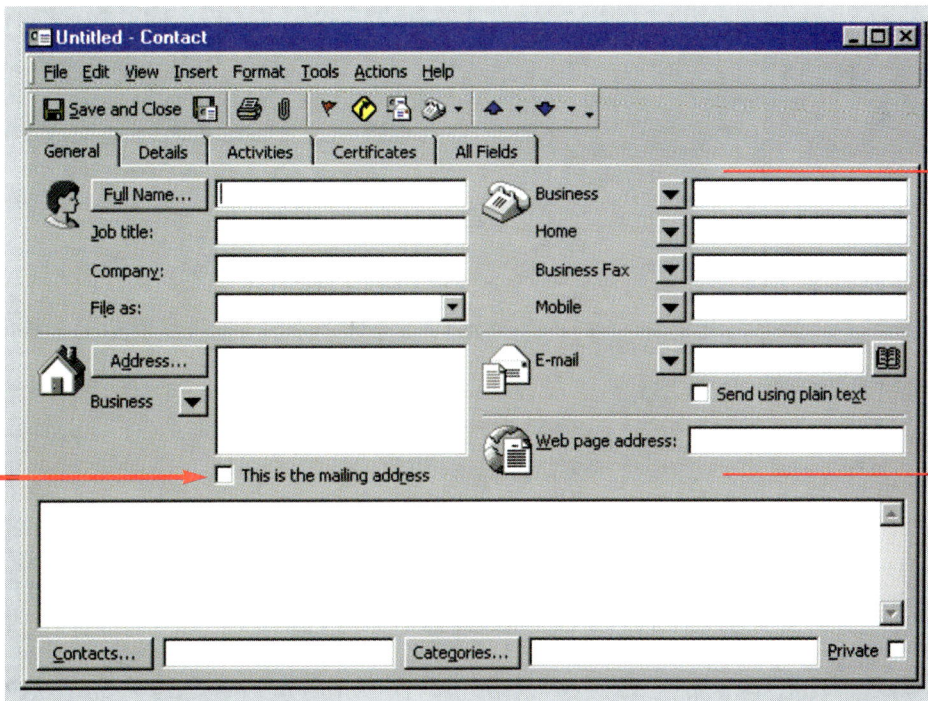

Make sure
this box is
checked
before
proceeding

Information
about contacts
will be entered
in these boxes

Figure 4-2 Categories dialog box

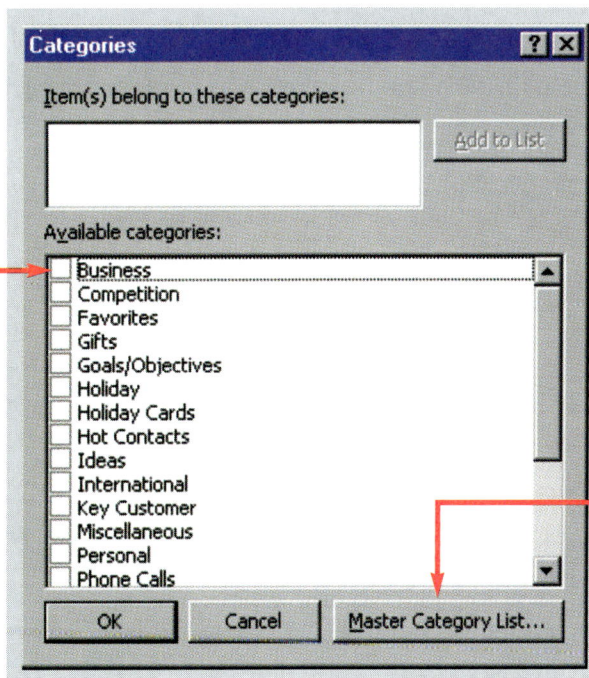

Click in the
boxes to apply
the categories to
the contacts

Click here
to change
the master
category list

Skill

Creating and Deleting Contacts (continued)

Do It!

12 Your Contact form should now look like **Figure 4-3**.

13 Click 🖫 Save and Close on the Contact form. The Contact card for Jon Walters now appears in the Information viewer (**Figure 4-4**).

14 Click once on the Address Card for Abner Adams.

15 Click the [Delete] button ☒ on the Standard toolbar to delete the contact.

More

There are up to three folders in which to organize your contact information depending on the configuration you chose when you installed Outlook 2000. If you are using the Corporate/Workgroup configuration, the Global Address Book contains the list of people in your network. Generally a network administrator maintains this list. In either the Corporate/Workgroup or Internet Only configurations, the Outlook Address Book contains your contacts and you add contacts to your Contact list. In the Internet Only configuration you also have a Personal Address book.

If you are using Outlook in the Corporate/Workgroup environment and would like to add a Personal Address Book, click Tools, and then click Services. In the Services dialog box, on the Services tab, click the Add button. In the Add Services to Profile dialog box, select Personal Address Book from the Available information services scroll box. Finally, click OK .

Additionally, it is possible to create a new Contact form out of an e-mail. Begin by clicking once on the e-mail you wish to convert. Then, click and drag the e-mail from the Inbox to the Contacts icon in either the Outlook Bar or the Folder List. Outlook will automatically open a Contact form with information gleaned from the e-mail. You can also right-click the name you want to make into a contact in the From field on an open e-mail message. Select the Add to Contacts command from the shortcut menu to open the new Contact form.

You can copy information that is the same from an existing contact to a new Contact form. Select the contact you want to copy. Open the Actions menu and select the New Contact from Same Company command. Most of the pertinent company information such as the company name, business address, and telephone and fax numbers will be copied to the new Contact form. Enter the Full Name and other information and click 🖫 Save and Close .

The Contact form also contains a field for entering the Web page address of your business contacts. When you enter the URL it becomes a hyperlink, which you can use to quickly and easily visit the Web sites of your contacts. However, the Web site address will not be copied when you use the New Contact from Same Company command, so you will have to reenter it.

Figure 4-3 Completed Contact form

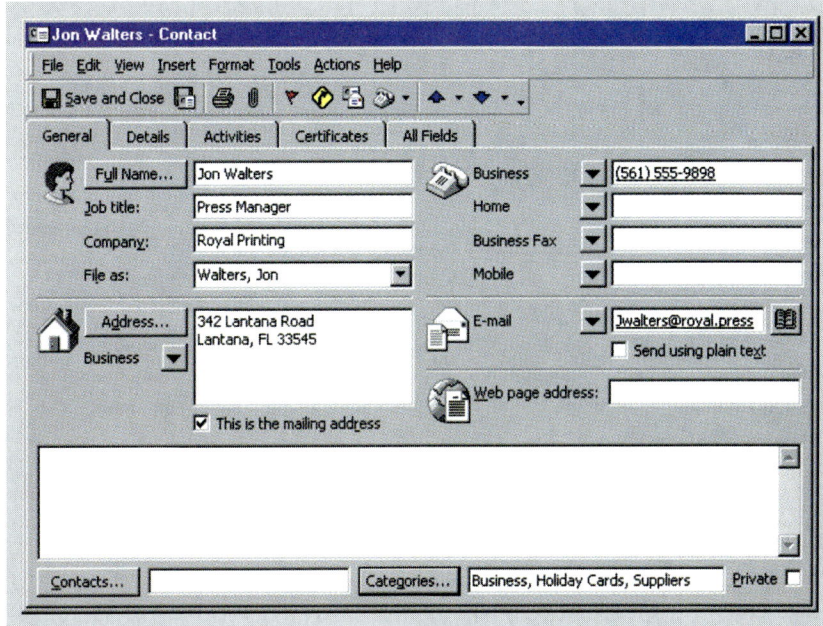

Figure 4-4 Contacts Information viewer in Address Cards view

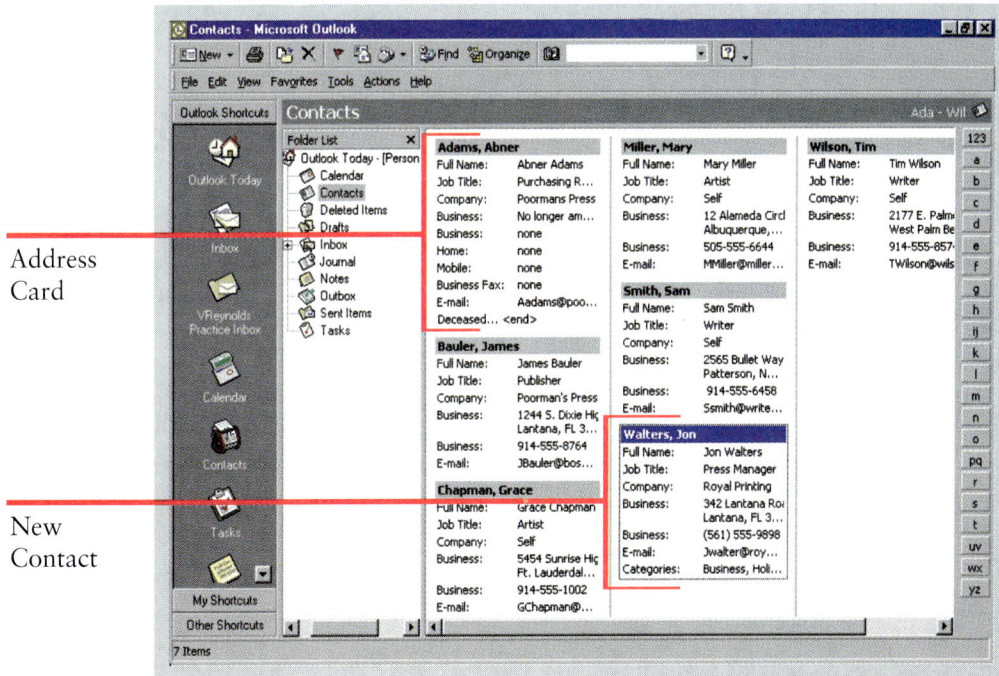

Address
Card

New
Contact

Practice

Open **Prac 4-1** in the Practice Files folder. Print the practice file and follow the directions.

Hot Tip

If you have more than one contact to add to your Outlook Address Book, you can click the **Save and New** button ▣. This will save the first contact and bring up a new Contact form.

Skill ## Editing Contacts

Concept

As you become more familiar with your contacts, you will learn additional information about them. You may need to add extra detail to your Contacts list or change existing data. A contact's position, job title or phone number may change, or you may want to add their assistant or spouse's name or their birthday. It is easy to keep your contact base accurate and updated using Outlook 2000.

Do It!

Virginia has been given more information about one of her contacts and will now add it to the Contact form.

1 The Contacts Information viewer should be on your screen. If it is not, click 📖 in the Outlook Bar.

2 Double-click James Bauler's name in the Contacts Information viewer.

3 When the James Bauler Contact form appears (**Figure 4-5**), click the Details tab.

4 Type Owner in the Department text box.

5 Type Virginia Reynolds in the Assistant's name text box.

6 Type Boss in the Nickname text box.

7 Type Bobbi Bauler in the Spouse's name text box.

8 Click down-arrow button in the Anniversary list box and select the nearest June 4.

9 Your Contact form should now resemble **Figure 4-6**. Click 💾 Save and Close to update the contact.

More

To edit a field you have already entered simply click in the field, use the Backspace and Delete keys to remove the necessary characters, and retype or correct the entry.

There are three more tabs in the Contact form: Activities, Certificates, and All Fields. The Activities tab lists all occurrences of this contact's name within the Outlook program. All incoming or outgoing e-mail, notes, tasks and appointments containing the contact's name will be listed. The Certificates tab allows you to encrypt e-mail and documents that you send to this contact. In the All Fields tab you can add additional information to the Contact form such as children's names, hobbies, and alternative addresses. If the field you want to include is not in the list, select All Contact fields from the Select from list box and click the New button at the bottom of the Contact form. Enter the new field name in the New Field dialog box and click OK.

Figure 4-5 James Bauler Contact form

Click one of
these tabs
to add more
detail about
the contact

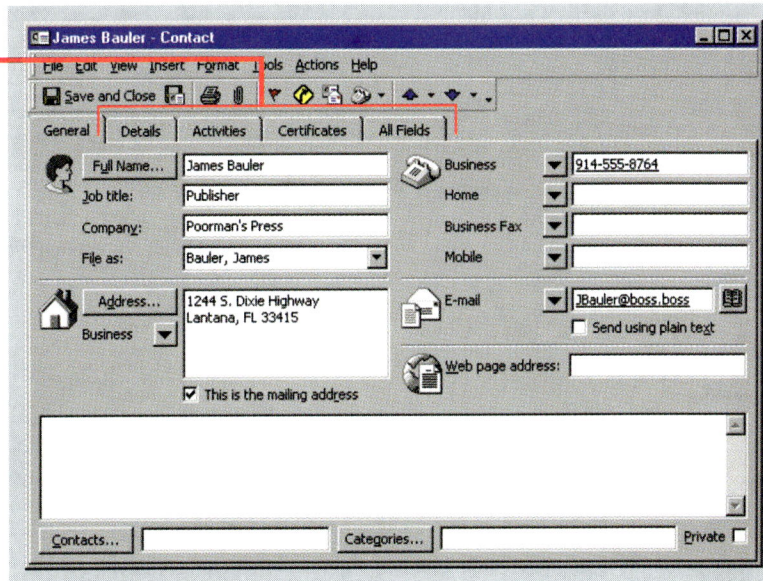

Figure 4-6 Completed Contact form

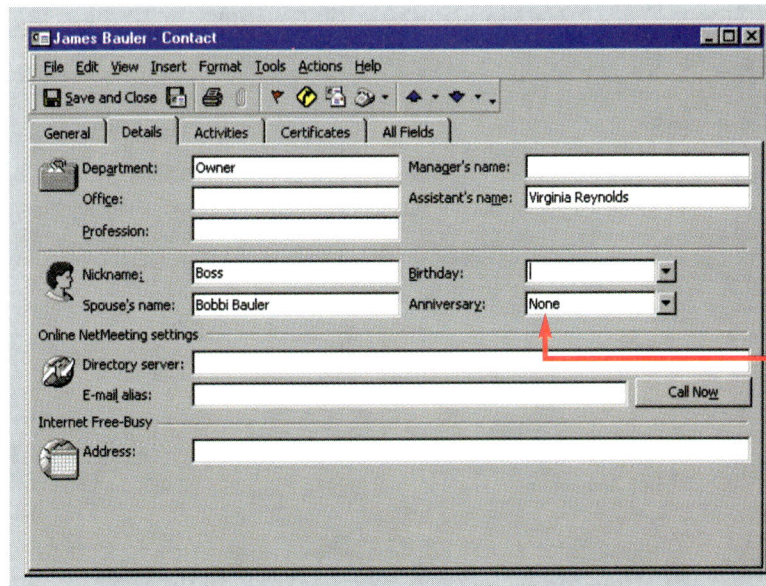

The date on
your form will
be different

Practice

Open the **Prac 4-2** file in the Practice Files folder. Print the file and follow the directions.

Hot Tip

You can use the Previous Item and Next Item buttons on the Contact form's Standard toolbar to move between contacts. The button will access the previous contact and he button will access the next contact.

Skill Organizing Contacts

Concept

When you open the Contacts folder, the Contact's Information viewer opens in Address Cards view by default. However, you can reorganize your contacts using the various views to quickly and efficiently locate the information you need. For example, you can switch to Phone List view to locate a phone number or to By Company view to find a contact from a particular company.

Do It!

Virginia has received information that one of her contacts is no longer available. She will delete that contact and then organize the remaining contacts.

1. The Contacts Information viewer should be on your screen. If it is not, click 📷 on the Outlook Bar.

2. Click once on Tim Wilson in the Contacts Information viewer.

3. Press the [Delete] key. Tim Wilson is removed from your list of contacts and placed in the Deleted Items folder.

4. Click the View button on the Menu bar.

5. Rest the mouse pointer over Current View.

6. From the submenu, click By Category.

7. Your screen should now look like **Figure 4-7**. Click on the (+) next to Categories: Holiday Cards.

8. The category will open, revealing those contacts who are assigned to the Holiday Cards category (**Figure 4-8**).

9. Close the category by clicking on the (-) next to Categories: Holiday Cards.

More

To return to the default view, open the View menu, highlight Current View, and click Address Cards.

In addition to the Address Cards, Phone List and Category views, you can choose Detailed Address Cards, By Company, By Location, or By Follow-up Flag view. By Location view will sort the contacts list by geographic location. Follow-up Flag view will group the contacts by their flag status. You can flag a contact to remind yourself to arrange a follow-up meeting or phone call, or to send a follow-up e-mail or letter. By Follow-up Flag view will group your contacts to display flagged contacts first, contacts with a completed follow-up action second, and regular contacts last.

Figure 4-7 Contacts organized by category

Click the plus sign to view the contents of the category

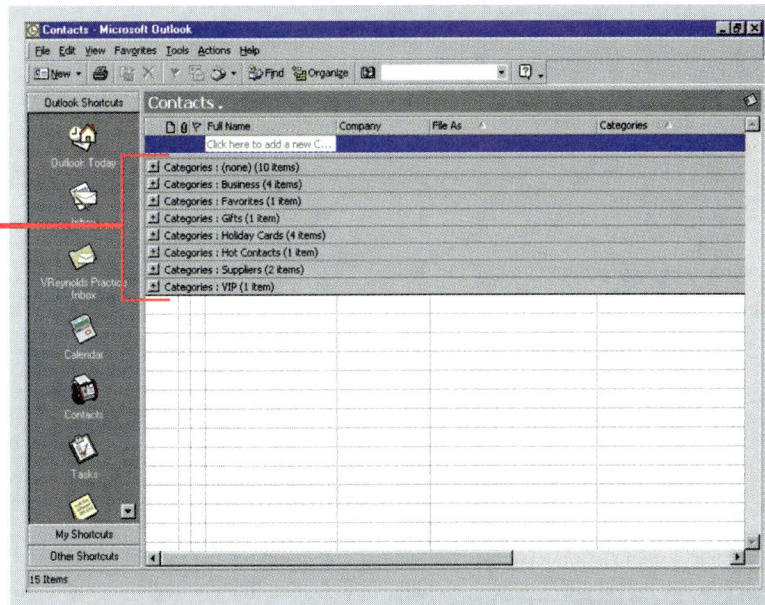

Figure 4-8 Holiday Cards category

Click minus sign to close category

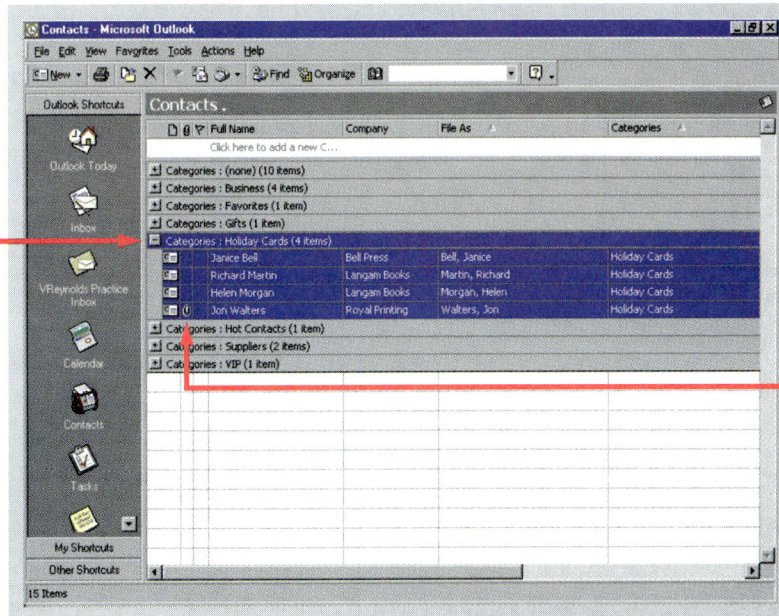

This icon indicates that there is a task associated with this person

Practice

View your contacts by the following:
1. **Phone List**
2. **By Location**
3. **By Company**
Before moving on to the next skill, return the view to **Address Cards**.

Hot Tip

Clicking Detailed Address Cards will expand the normal address card to include the contact's company name, job title, and department.

OL 4.9

Skill

Sending Contact Information by E-Mail

Concept

You can send information about your contacts to other individuals using the Vcard. The Vcard is an electronic business card that contains all the information entered in the Contact form. You can share contact information with business associates or send your own virtual business card as an e-mail attachment.

Do It!

A co-worker has asked Virginia to send her a Vcard for the owner of their publishing firm.

1 The Contacts Information viewer should be on your screen. If it is not, click 🖿 on the Outlook Bar.

2 Click the ▾ button button next to the ☐New ▾ button on the Standard toolbar. Select the Mail Message command from the menu.

3 On the Untitled Message form, type: Kroan@Poormans.press in the To: text box.

4 Click in the Subject text box and type: The Boss's Card. Press the [Enter] key.

5 In the message area, type: Here is all the information I have on the boss, Kay. Press the [Enter] key twice.

6 Open the Insert menu on the Message form and select the Item command. The Insert Item dialog box will open.

7 In the Look in scroll box (**Figure 4-9**) click Contacts.

8 Select Bauler, James in the Items scroll box.

9 Make sure the Attachment radio button is selected in the Insert as section and click ☐ OK ☐ .

10 When you see your original e-mail message with the Vcard at the bottom (**Figure 4-10**), click ☐Send .

More

A Vcard is also an excellent way to share information about yourself. Using a new Contact form, enter all the information you would like to share with other business people and save it as you usually would. Now you can attach it to introductory letters to give new contacts your complete profile without having to retype all the information each time.

A colleague must be using Outlook, Outlook Express, Netscape Messenger or another compatible program in order to receive a Vcard. If your business associate does not use a compatible program, you can save a Contact card as a text file using the Save As command on the File menu. Attach the file to an e-mail message using the File command on the Insert menu.

Figure 4-9 Insert Item dialog box

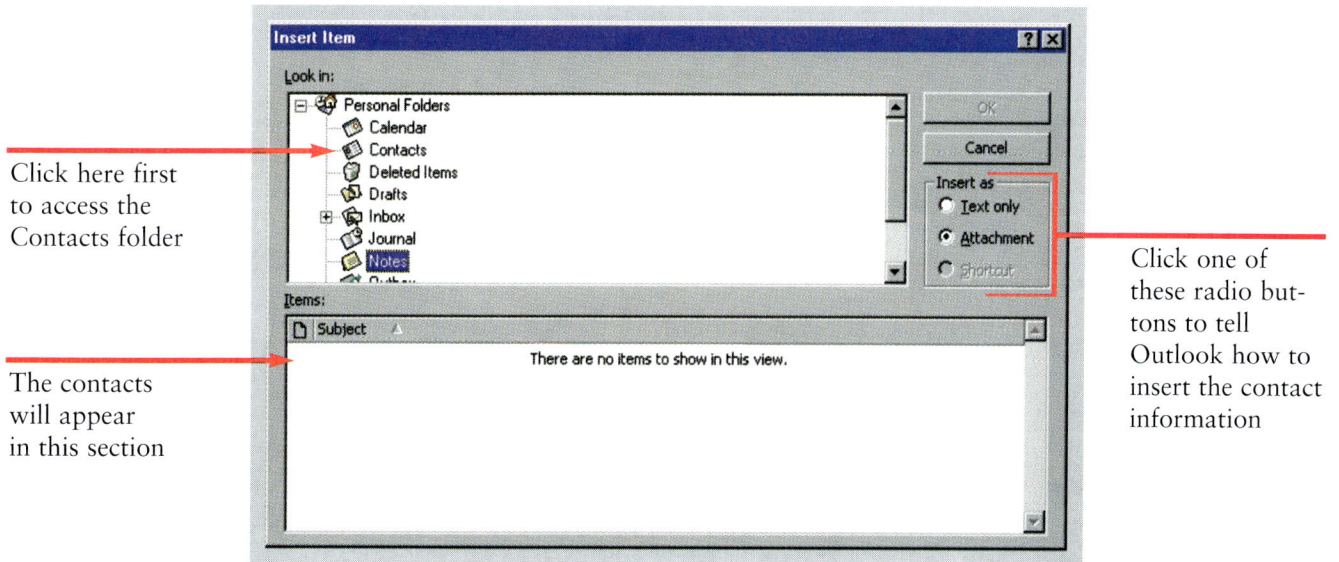

Click here first
to access the
Contacts folder

The contacts
will appear
in this section

Click one of
these radio but-
tons to tell
Outlook how to
insert the contact
information

Figure 4-10 Completed e-mail

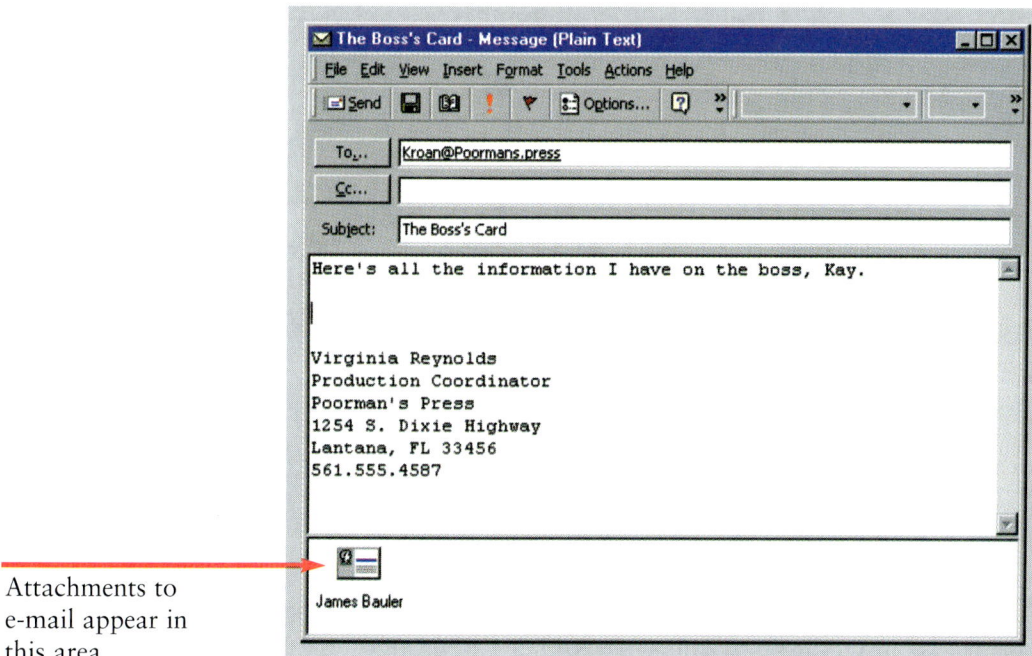

Attachments to
e-mail appear in
this area

Practice

Make a Vcard for yourself, and attach it to
an e-mail introducing yourself to
Jbauler@Poormans.press.

Hot Tip

To quickly access a new **Message form**
while in the Contacts folder, press
[Ctrl]+[Shift]+[M].

Skill   Creating Tasks

Concept

You can keep track of all the jobs you must complete and follow the progress of ongoing projects using the Tasks folder. When you create tasks, Outlook becomes an electronic project manager. You can maximize your job efficiency by setting deadlines and reminders and creating recurring tasks.

Do It!

Virginia will create a task concerning the L7 books.

1. Open the Outlook program and click the Tasks shortcut 📋 on the Outlook Bar. The Tasks Information viewer appears.

2. Click the New Task button ☑ New ▾ on the Tasks Standard toolbar. A new blank Task form with the default name Untitled appears (**Figure 4-11**).

3. Type: Check on L7 Illustrations in the Subject text box.

4. Click ↻ Recurrence... on the Task form's Standard toolbar.

5. The Task Recurrence dialog box opens (**Figure 4-12**). In the Recurrence pattern section, click the Weekly radio button.

6. Click the Monday check box.

7. Click the Regenerate new task radio button.

8. Click OK at the bottom of the dialog box.

9. Click 🖫 Save and Close on the Check on L7 Illustration Task form. The task is now added to your Tasks list.

More

You have just created a recurring task. Each time you check the task off as completed, another task will be generated that is due in one week. Click the Completion box in the Tasks list to designate that a task is complete. To create one-time tasks, do not use the Recurrence button.

In this exercise you learned how to add a task in the Tasks folder. If you want to add just a simple task and its description, you can enter it on the TaskPad in the Calendar folder. Tasks appear in alphabetical order on the TaskPad. When they are overdue, they appear in red.

You can also designate whether a task is High, Low or Normal priority in the Priority list box, and set a reminder date and time in the Reminder list boxes on the Task form.

It is possible to create a task from an e-mail that you receive. For example, you receive an e-mail asking you to track a project. Drag the e-mail from the Inbox to the Tasks icon. A Task form will open with the subject of the e-mail as the task. Add the remaining information to the form and save and close it. It is now a task.

Figure 4-11 Blank Task form

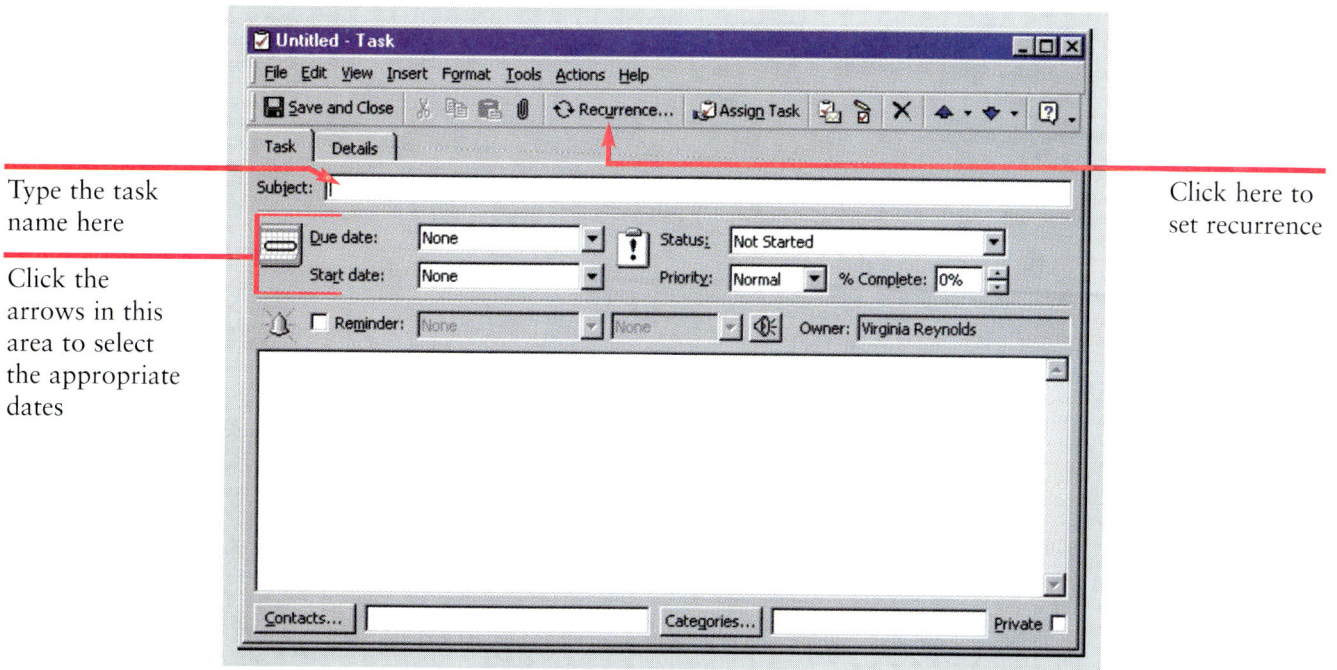

Type the task name here

Click the arrows in this area to select the appropriate dates

Click here to set recurrence

Figure 4-12 Task Recurrence dialog box

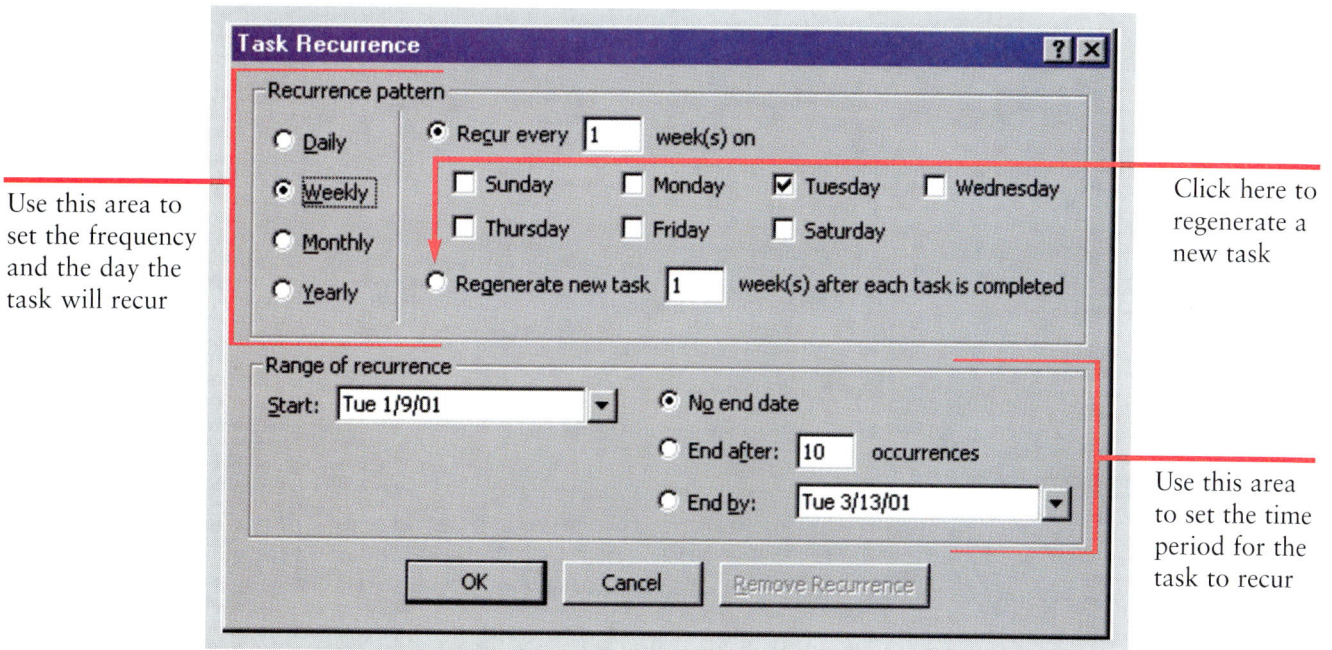

Use this area to set the frequency and the day the task will recur

Click here to regenerate a new task

Use this area to set the time period for the task to recur

Practice

Open the student practice file, **Prac 4-3** and follow the directions.

Hot Tip

To quickly generate a new **Task form**, press **[Ctrl]+[N]** while in the Tasks folder.

Skill Assigning Tasks

Concept

You may need to assign a task to a colleague or a subordinate. Outlook allows you to create a task and assign it to another individual in your workgroup or over the Internet. You can also request automatic updates and a report when the task is complete.

Do It!

Virginia will create a task and assign it to an artist.

1. If the Tasks folder is not open, click 📋 on the Outlook Bar.

2. Open the File menu, highlight New, and select the Task Request command from the submenu.

3. On the Task Request form that appears, (**Figure 4-13**) Type: Mary Miller in the To: text box.

4. Type: Chapter 6 Illustrations in the Subject text box.

5. In the Due Date list box, click ▼ and select the date three weeks from today.

6. In the Start Date list box, click ▼ and select today's date.

7. Click ▼ in the Status list box and select In Progress.

8. If they are not checked, click the appropriate check boxes to Keep an updated copy of this task on my task list and to Send me a status report when this task is complete.

9. Click in the Message section of the Task Request form and type: Mary, Can you complete the illustrations by this deadline? Ginny.

10. Click 🖃 Send and Outlook will send the task request and automatically add a copy of the task to your task list (**Figure 4-14**).

More

Once you assign a task, you do not own it anymore. In other words, any changes that you attempt to make to that task will not show up in the assignee's copy of the task. Therefore, you should strive to be very accurate when assigning tasks to others.

You can also assign a task to multiple people, but you will not be able to receive automatic status reports. If the person you assign the task to is not connected to you through a network, he or she will receive the Task Request as an ordinary e-mail without the Accept and Decline buttons. You will not be able to receive automatic updates when you assign tasks via the Internet.

Figure 4-13 Task Request form

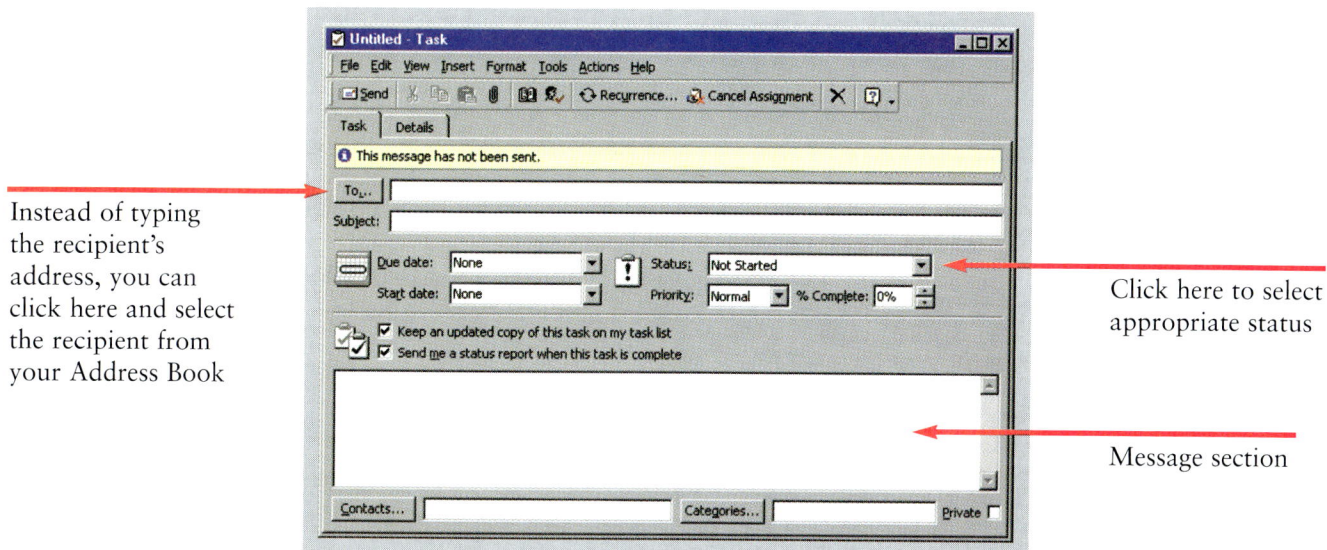

Instead of typing the recipient's address, you can click here and select the recipient from your Address Book

Click here to select appropriate status

Message section

Figure 4-14 Updated Task list

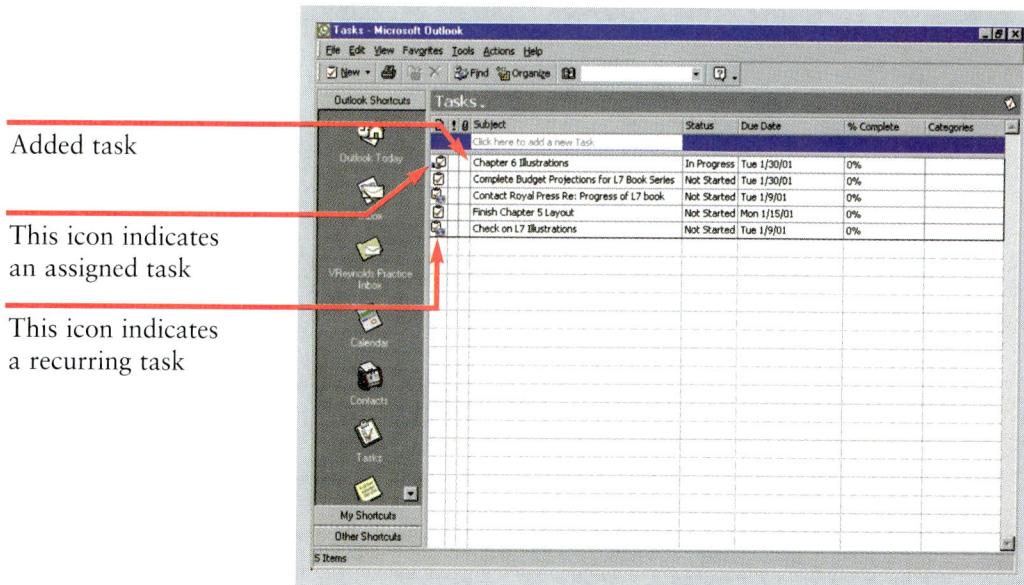

Added task

This icon indicates an assigned task

This icon indicates a recurring task

Practice

Open the student practice file, **Prac 4-4** and follow the directions.

Hot Tip

You can turn an existing task into a task request by double-clicking on the task, and then clicking the **Assign Task** button on the Task form's Standard toolbar.

Skill

Accepting and Declining Tasks

Concept

Superiors or co-workers can also assign tasks to you. You must decide to accept, decline, or reassign a task quickly because you are the temporary "owner" of the task and no one else can make changes to it. If you accept a task it is automatically placed on your Tasks list and the person who assigned it to you can receive automatic updates. If you decline a task it is returned to the sender.

Do It!

Virginia will accept one task from her boss, but will decline another.

1. For this lesson, you must install the Practice Tasks files. See Lesson 1 for information on how to do this. Install the Practice Tasks files to the VReynolds Practice Inbox.

2. Click 🖂 on the Outlook Bar.

3. Double-click the Task Request titled: Aspen Convention from James Bauler. A Task Request form opens (**Figure 4-15**).

4. Read the message. Open the Actions menu on the Task Request form and select the Reply command.

5. Type: Boss: Will do. Virginia on the Reply form.

6. Click 🖃 Send. The message is sent and the Reply form disappears.

7. Click the Accept button ✓ Accept on the Task Request form's Standard toolbar. The task is added to your Tasks list and the next Task Request form appears. (If it does not, double-click the next Task Request by James Bauler.)

8. Read the message and open a Reply form.

9. Type: Boss: Sorry, too busy. Can you get Karen to do it? Virginia.

10. Click 🖃 Send. The message is sent and the Reply form disappears.

11. Click the Decline button ✕ Decline on the Task Request form Standard toolbar. The Task Request form disappears.

12. Click 🗹 on the Outlook Bar. The Aspen Convention task has been added to your Tasks list because you accepted it, but that the Pay Schedule task has not been added because you declined it (**Figure 4-16**).

More

After you have accepted a task, you can also manually send updates. Double-click the task to access the Task form. Open the Actions menu and click the Send Status Report command. A Task Status Report form will be generated with some sections already filled in. You can alter any or all of the status report and send it to the person who assigned you the task.

Figure 4-15 Aspen Convention Task Request form

Accept or decline task here

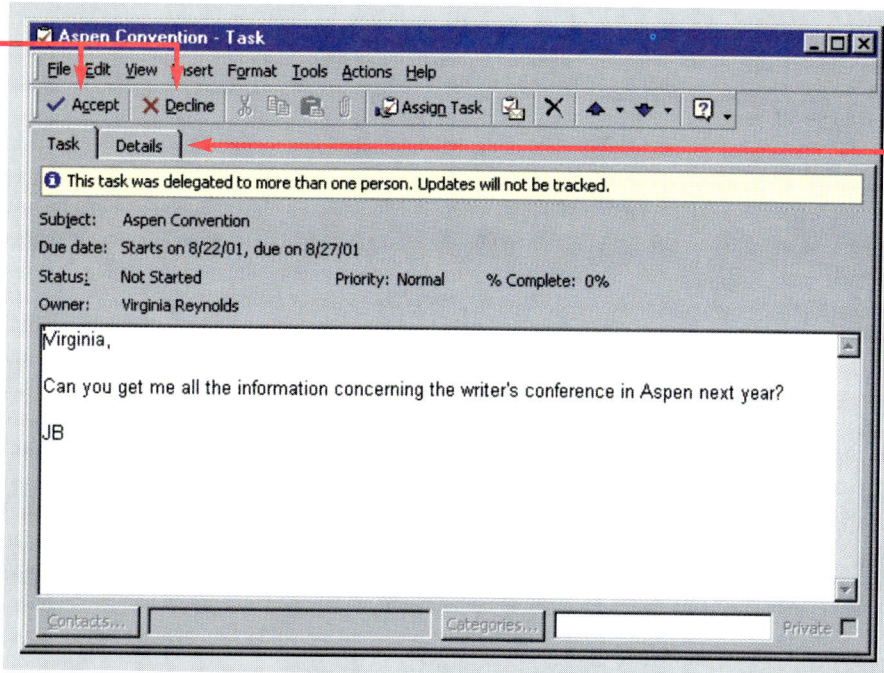

Click this tab for more details, if any, about the task

Figure 4-16 Updated Task list

This is the task you accepted

This icon indicates that the task was assigned to you by another person

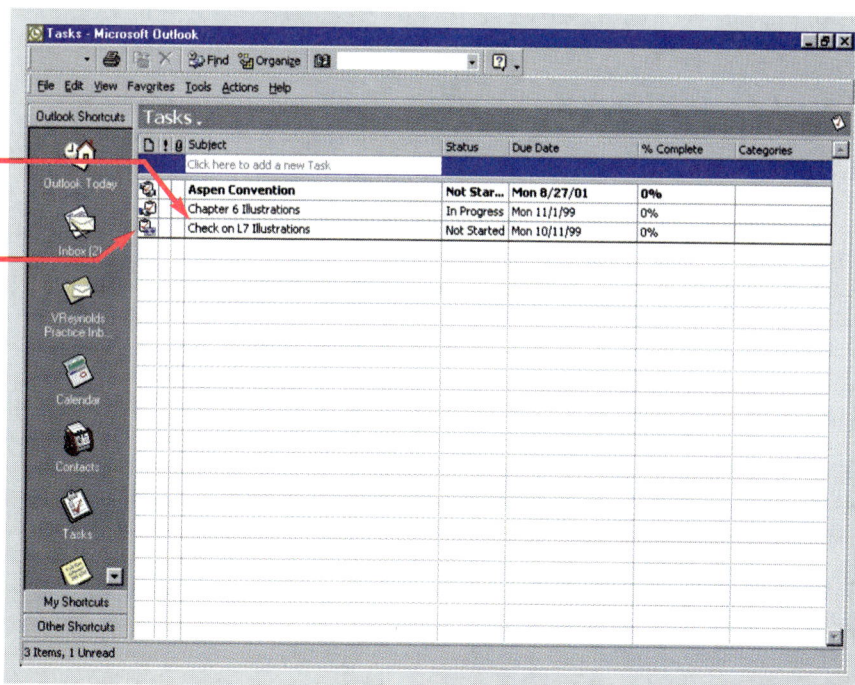

Practice

There are four task requests remaining in the Practice Inbox. Accept the tasks from **Helen Langam** and **Sam Smith**. Decline the tasks from **Thomas Singleton** and **James Bauler**. Send appropriate e-mails for all four tasks.

Hot Tip

If you accept a task by mistake, it is easy to delete it. Double-click the task to access the Task Request form. Open the Actions menu and select the Decline command.

Skill

Organizing Tasks

Concept

You can assign your tasks to a variety of categories in order to easily find, sort or group them. You also have many viewing options, which enable you to quickly locate specific tasks. After you organize your tasks you can easily find assignments associated with a specific project, or tasks listed in various categories such as Business or Personal.

Do It!

Virginia will organize her tasks by category and change the view of her Tasks list.

1. If the Tasks Information viewer is not on your screen, click 📋 on the Outlook Bar.

2. Click 🗂 Organize on the Standard toolbar. The Ways to Organize Tasks panel opens (**Figure 4-17**).

3. Click the Using Categories page.

4. Click the task titled: Meeting Information.

5. Click the ▼ button in the Add Tasks selected below to list box.

6. Click Personal and click the Add button. This task is now categorized as a Personal task.

7. Click the task titled: Merger and Taxes. Click ▼ in the Add Tasks selected below to list box and select Business. Click Add.

8. Follow the same procedure to add Aspen Convention to the Business category.

9. When you are finished, click ✕ in the upper-right corner of the Ways to Organize Tasks panel.

10. Open the View menu and highlight Current View. When the submenu opens, select the By Category command. Your screen should look like **Figure 4-18**.

11. Click the small plus sign (+) next to Business. The category expands to reveal the two business-related tasks. Click the small minus sign (-) to close the category. Click the (+) next to Personal to reveal the personal task.

More

You can also assign a task to a category when you create or accept the task. In the lower right-hand corner of the Task Request form, click the Categories button. In the Categories dialog box, select the check box for the appropriate category from the Available categories scroll box. Click OK to close the Categories dialog box. Now when you accept the task, or save and close it, it will automatically be assigned to the correct category.

Along with the Categories view discussed in this lesson, there are several other ways to view your tasks. To change your view in the Tasks Information viewer, open the View menu, highlight Current View, and then click on the view of your choice.

Figure 4-17 Ways to Organize Tasks panel

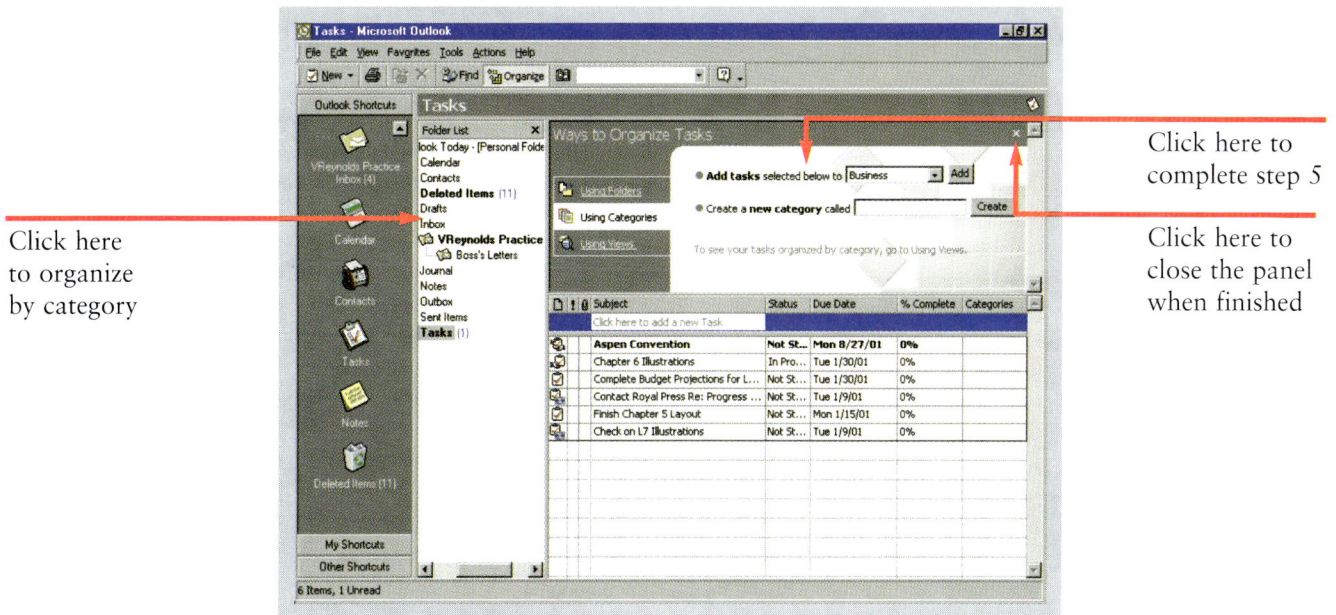

Click here
to organize
by category

Click here to
complete step 5

Click here to
close the panel
when finished

Figure 4-18 By Category view of tasks

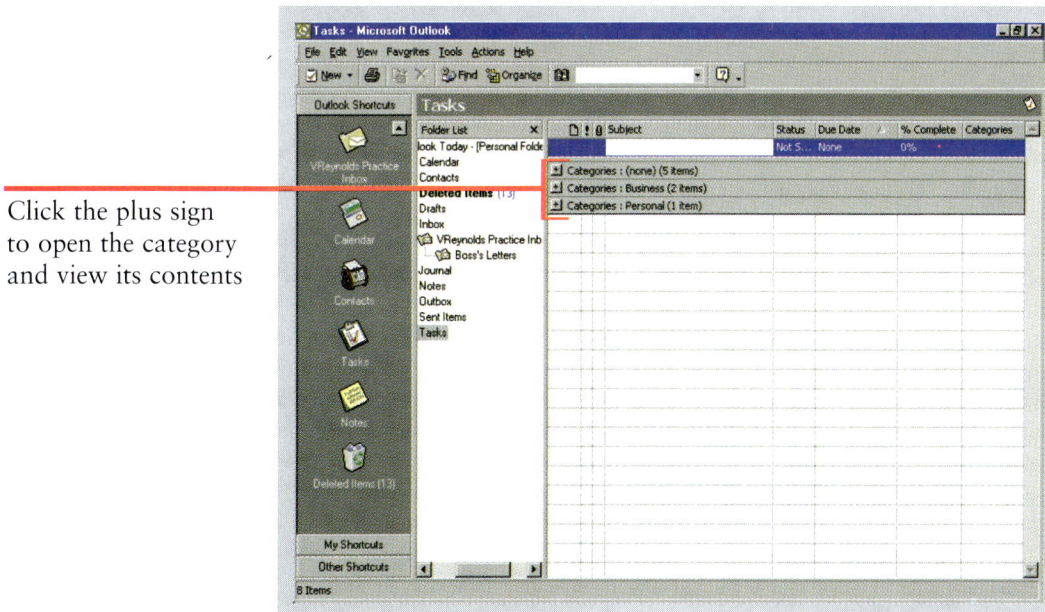

Click the plus sign
to open the category
and view its contents

Practice

Several tasks on your list have not been categorized. Categorize each of the tasks as either business or personal.

Hot Tip

If you want to see your tasks in list form, but wish to see the assigned categories as well, select **Detailed List** view from the **Current View** submenu.

Skill Creating and Editing Notes

Concept

You can create electronic sticky notes to serve as reminders or to record ideas or inspirations that you want to pursue. They can also be used to record questions you want to ask, directions to a convention site, or a specific business statistic. The great advantage of electronic notes is that you will not lose them in a disorganized jumble of paper.

Do It!

Virginia will create a note.

1 Click the Notes shortcut on the Outlook Bar to display the Notes Information viewer.

2 Click the New Note button on the Standard toolbar. A blank Note form will appear (**Figure 4-19**).

3 Type: Call Martha about taxes for the last fiscal year.

4 Click the Close button ⊠ on the Note form. The note disappears and an icon appears in the Notes Information viewer with the first few words of the note below it (**Figure 4-20**).

5 Double-click the note to make it reappear.

6 Place the insertion point after the period in the first sentence.

7 Press the [Enter] key twice.

8 Type: Martha: 555-6546.

9 Click ⊠ again.

More

If you minimize Outlook without minimizing a note, it will stay on your screen enabling you to view it while you use other Office applications.

To customize the appearance of a note, right-click the note in the Notes Information viewer to access a shortcut menu. Highlight Color to access a sub-menu listing the available color options. You can also forward a note to a colleague, print it out, or assign it to a category in the Categories dialog box.

The default note color is yellow. To change this, open the Tools menu and select the Options command to open the Options dialog box. Click the Note Options button to open the Note Options dialog box. Select the color you want from the Color list box. You can also adjust the note size in the Size list box or click the Font button to change the default font settings. Click [OK] to close each of the dialog boxes.

Figure 4-19 The electronic note

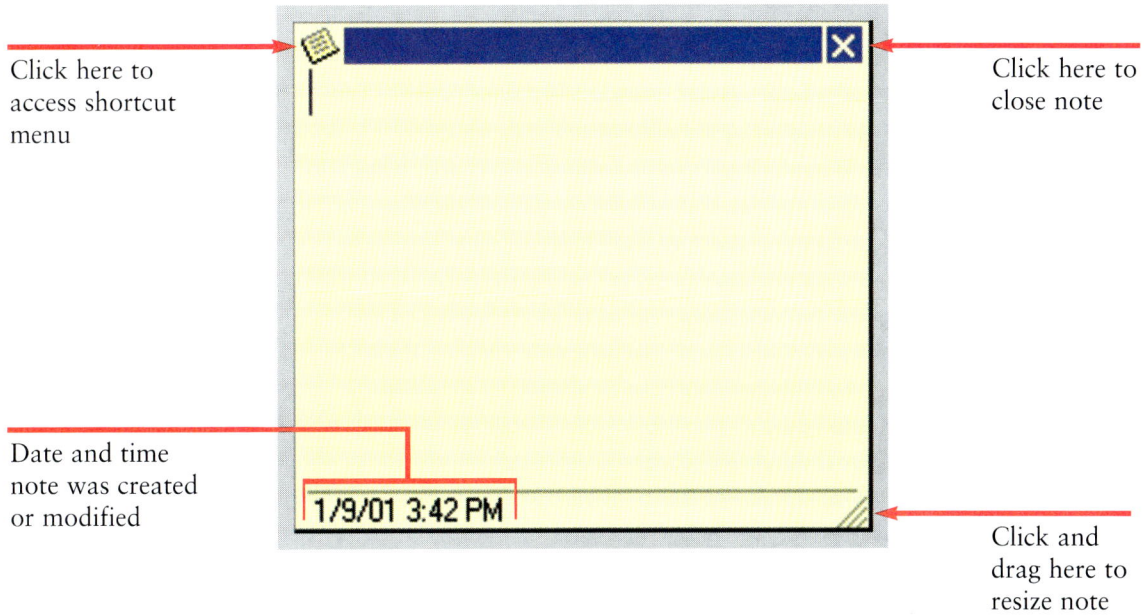

Click here to access shortcut menu

Click here to close note

Date and time note was created or modified

1/9/01 3:42 PM

Click and drag here to resize note

Figure 4-20 Notes interface

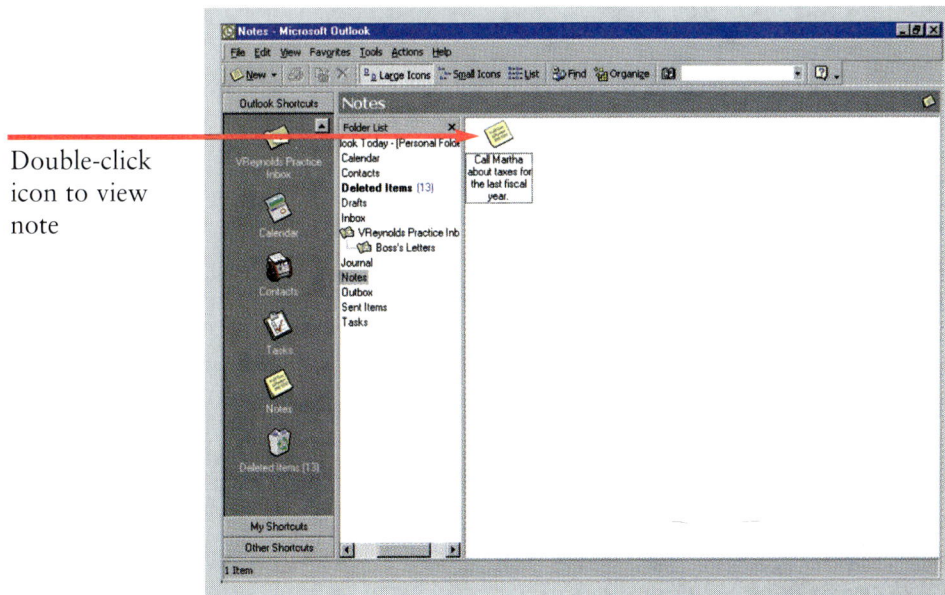

Double-click icon to view note

Practice

Create ten notes of your choice and practice opening, closing, customizing and forwarding them.

Hot Tip

To delete a note, right-click it, and select the **Delete** command from the shortcut menu.

Skill Organizing and Viewing Notes

Concept

Electronic notes can be very like handwritten notes in one respect; they can accumulate. While most people don't organize their handwritten notes, using Outlook you can organize your notes using several different views. You can list them sorted by creation date, or list only notes created in the last seven days. You can also color-code them to organize them into various subjects or categories.

Do It!

Virginia will color-code her notes and change the view to sort her Notes folder by color.

1 If the Notes Information viewer is not on your screen, click ▨ on the Outlook Bar.

2 Click ▨New▾.

3 Type: Call Sam about model builders meeting. Click the Note icon in the upper-left corner of the Note form (**Figure 4-21**).

4 Highlight Color on the shortcut menu and select Pink for personal notes.

5 Click ✖ to close the Note form.

6 Press [Ctrl]+[N] to open a new, blank Note form.

7 Type: Talk to Boss about new book idea. Click the Note icon.

8 Highlight Color on the shortcut menu and choose Blue for business notes. Close the Note form.

9 Open the View menu, highlight Current View, and select the By Color command.

10 Your notes are listed by color as shown in **Figure 4-22**. To view the notes in each category, click the small plus sign button (+). Double-click a note to review it.

More

In Icons view your notes will be displayed as icons arranged from left to right by creation date. Notes view will display your notes in a list sorted by creation date. Last Seven Days view will enable you to access a list of the notes you created in the last week. Finally, you can assign categories to notes just as you did with tasks, and view them By Category.

Figure 4-21 Notes shortcut menus

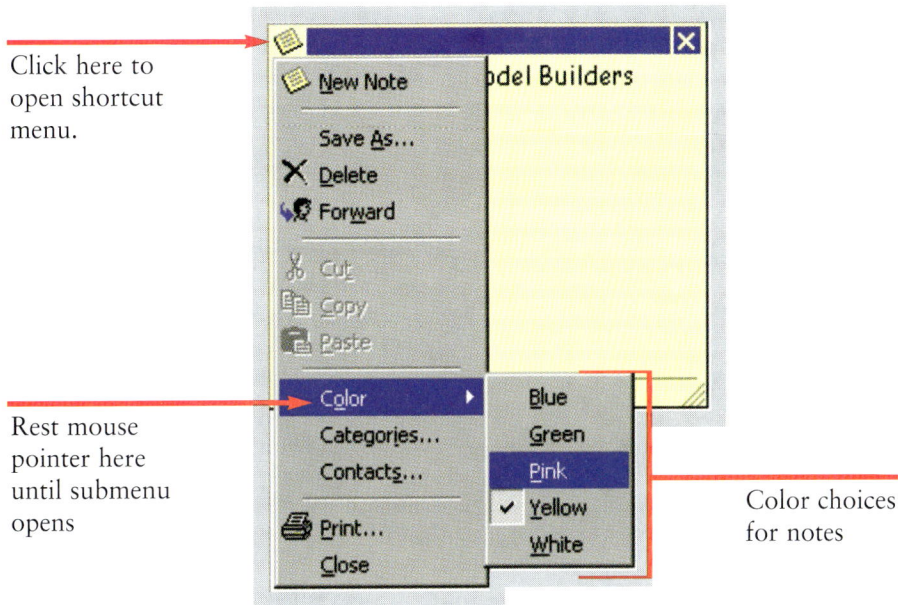

Click here to open shortcut menu.

New Note

Save As...

Delete

Forward

Cut

Copy

Paste

Color ▶

Categories...

Contacts...

Print...

Close

Blue

Green

Pink

Yellow

White

del Builders

Rest mouse pointer here until submenu opens

Color choices for notes

Figure 4-22 Notes organized by color

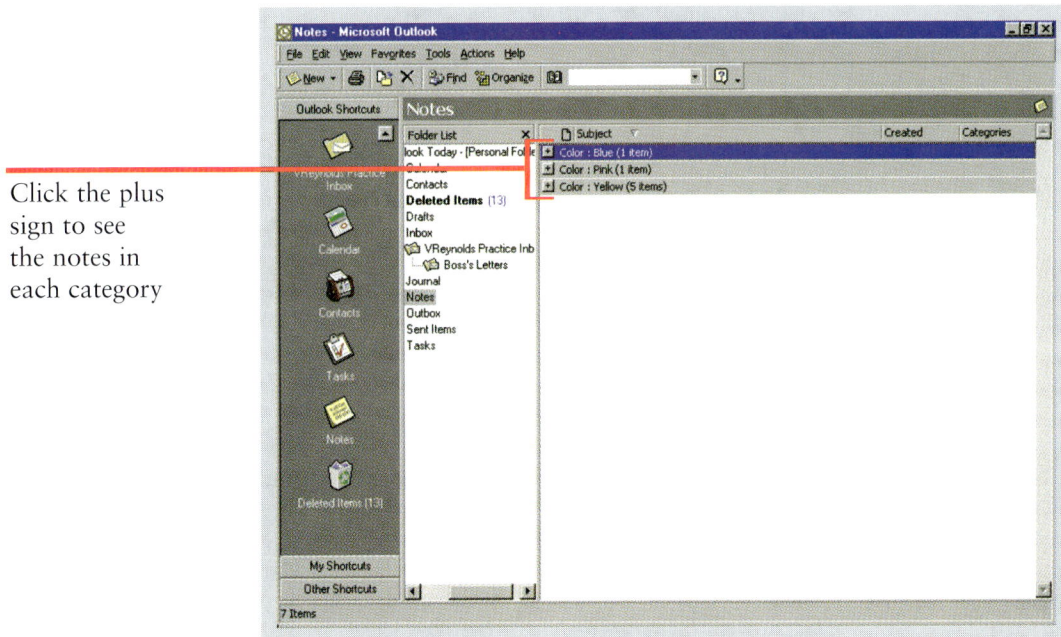

Click the plus sign to see the notes in each category

Practice

Create ten notes, five business and five personal, and color-code them appropriately.

Hot Tip

You can print a note by opening the note and pressing **[Ctrl]+[P]**.

Skill

Creating Journal Entries

Concept

The Outlook Journal can be used to track certain items you create within the program including e-mail messages, meeting requests and responses, and task requests. You can also automatically track activity related to the documents you create using Microsoft Office, such as letters, memos, or reports from Word, spreadsheets from Excel, databases from Access, or presentations created with PowerPoint. You can specify which items you want the Journal to automatically track, or manually enter items that cannot be automatically tracked such as appointments, tasks and notes.

Do It!

Virginia will manually enter an activity in the Journal.

1. With the Outlook program running and the Folder List active, click the Journal shortcut on the My Shortcuts Bar.

2. The first time you open the Journal, the Office Assistant (if it is active) or a warning dialog box will inform you that the Journal can automatically track Microsoft Office documents and e-mail associated with a contact. It will also inform you that the Activities tab on the Contact card is the best way to track e-mail and does not require the Journal. Click [Yes] to turn the Journal on.

3. The Journal Options dialog box may open. Click [OK] to close the dialog box and, if necessary, click [OK] to close the Options dialog box.

4. Click 📇 on the Outlook Bar (or in the Folder List) to open the Contacts folder.

5. Click and drag Grace Chapman's Address card to the Journal icon on the Outlook Bar or in the Folder List.

6. A Journal Entry form will open (**Figure 4-23**). Ensure that today's date is showing in the Start Time box. Click ▾ in the Time box and select 9:00 AM.

7. In the Duration box, click ▾ and select 10 minutes. Click [💾 Save and Close]

8. Click the Journal shortcut on the My Shortcuts Bar. Click the [+] sign next to Entry Type: Phone Call. The Journal activity will be represented on the Journal timeline by a telephone icon with a clock as in **Figure 4-24**.

More

E-mail related activities are already automatically tracked for every contact in the Contacts folder. The Activities tab of each Contact card lists all incoming and outgoing messages, including meeting requests and responses. When you select contact names and choose activities in the Journal Options dialog box you are programming Outlook to record them in the Journal as well. This is useful in cases where you want to be able to quickly view activities related to a key customer or client.

After you start tracking them, activities related to your Office documents will be recorded in the Journal. To view entries that are not currently displayed, use the scroll bars to advance the Journal timeline. Double-click an entry to view it. Double- click the shortcut icon in the Journal Entry form to open an Office document.

Figure 4-23 Journal Entry form

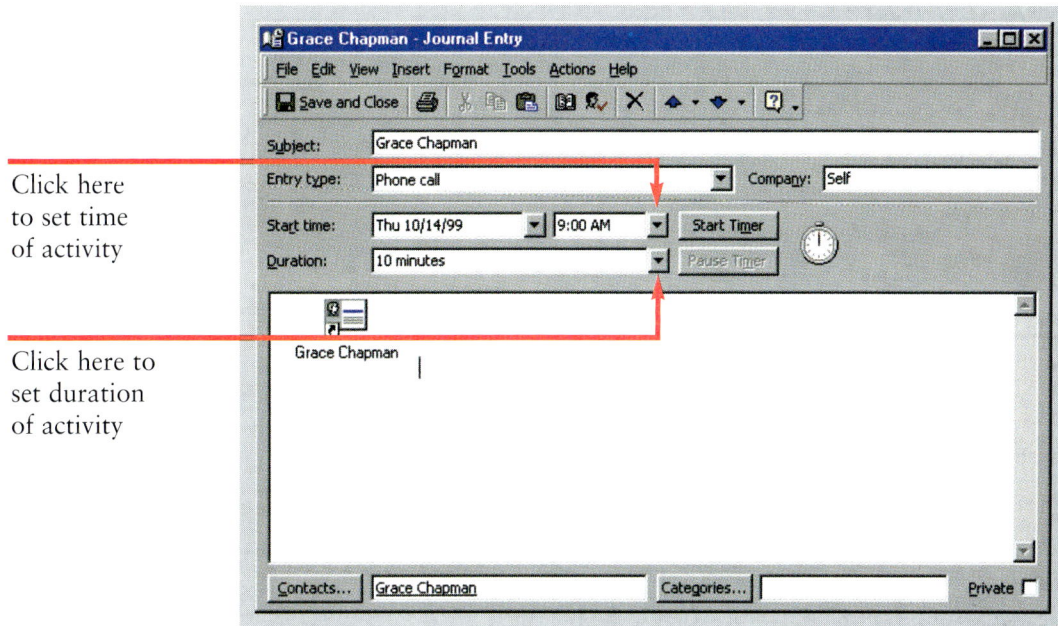

Click here
to set time
of activity

Click here to
set duration
of activity

Figure 4-24 Journal Entry

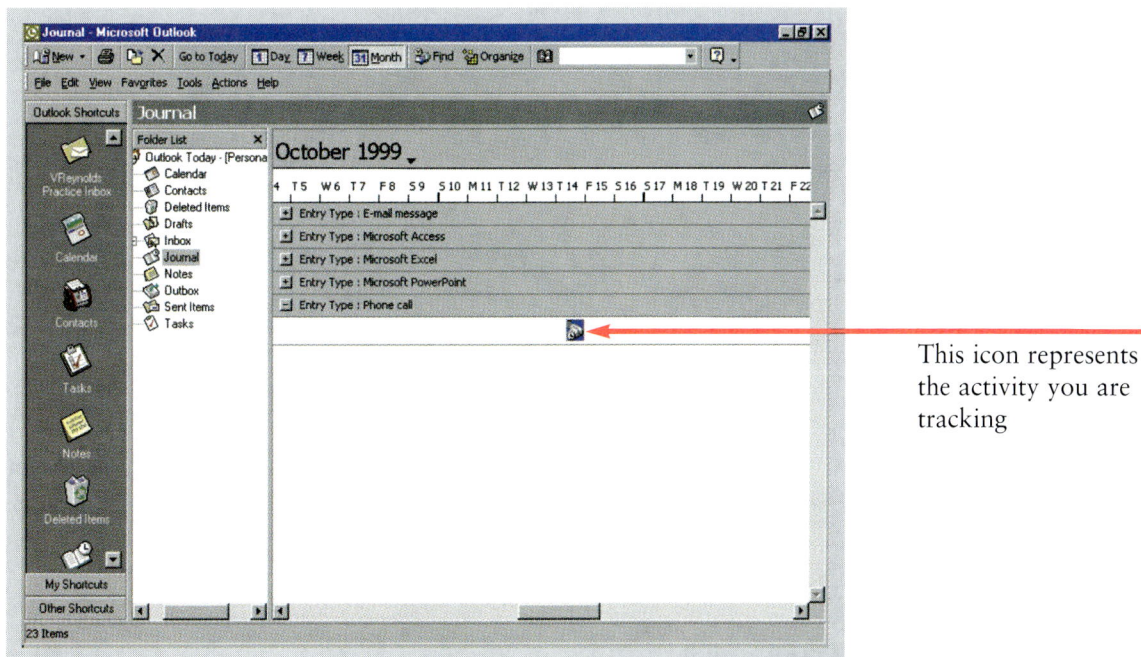

This icon represents
the activity you are
tracking

Practice

Create a Journal Entry for a fifteen minute
daily phone call with JBauler.

Hot Tip

A special contact icon with a small pencil
will precede Contacts whose activities you
have selected to be recorded in the
Journal.

Skill Integrating Outlook Components

Concept

Outlook functions well as separate components. The Calendar can be used independantly of the TaskPad, which can function separately from the Contacts list, etc. However, Outlook reaches its pinnacle of usefulness when its features are integrated into one cohesive unit.

Do It!

Virginia has received varied instructions from her supervisor. She will integrate several Outlook components to complete her tasks.

1 Click 📧 to open the VReynolds Practice Inbox.

2 Open the e-mail from JBauler entitled Random Thoughts.

3 The first task in the e-mail is to forward the new contact information. To begin, highlight the name and address of the contact using the click and drag method. The e-mail should look like Figure 4-25.

4 Click Edit on the Menu bar and click Copy to copy the information to the Office Clipboard. Close the Message form.

5 Click [New ▾] to open a new, blank Message form.

6 Address the e-mail to CMatha@accounting.net.

7 Type: Carl, Boss said you need to add this. Press the [Enter] key twice.

8 Open the Edit menu again, and click Paste. The information you copied from JBauler's e-mail is now pasted into the e-mail to CMatha. This e-mail should now look like Figure 4-26.

9 Click [Send].

10 Reopen JBauler's original e-mail. Press {Ctrl]+[Shift]+[C]. A new, untitled Contact form will appear.

11 Type Duncan Pfister's information into the Contact form. Move the Contact form by clicking and dragging if you cannot see all the information in the e-mail.

12 Click [Categories...]. Since Extremely Important Printer does not appear on the Category list, you will create it.

13 Click [Master Category List...]. When the Master Categories dialog box appears (Figure 4-27), type Extremely Important Printer.

Figure 4-25 Highlighted content

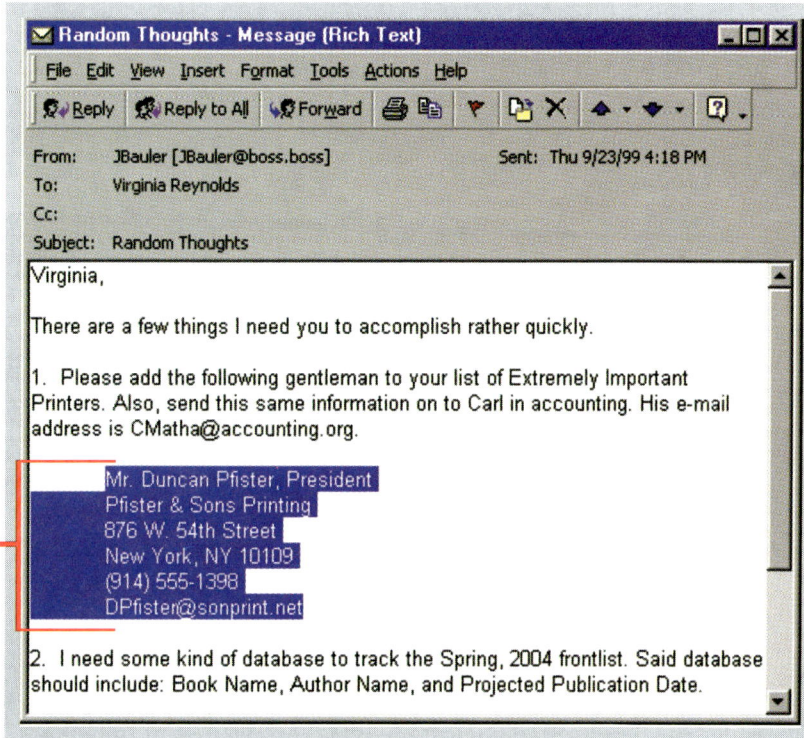

Properly
highlighted
text

Figure 4-26 Completed e-mail

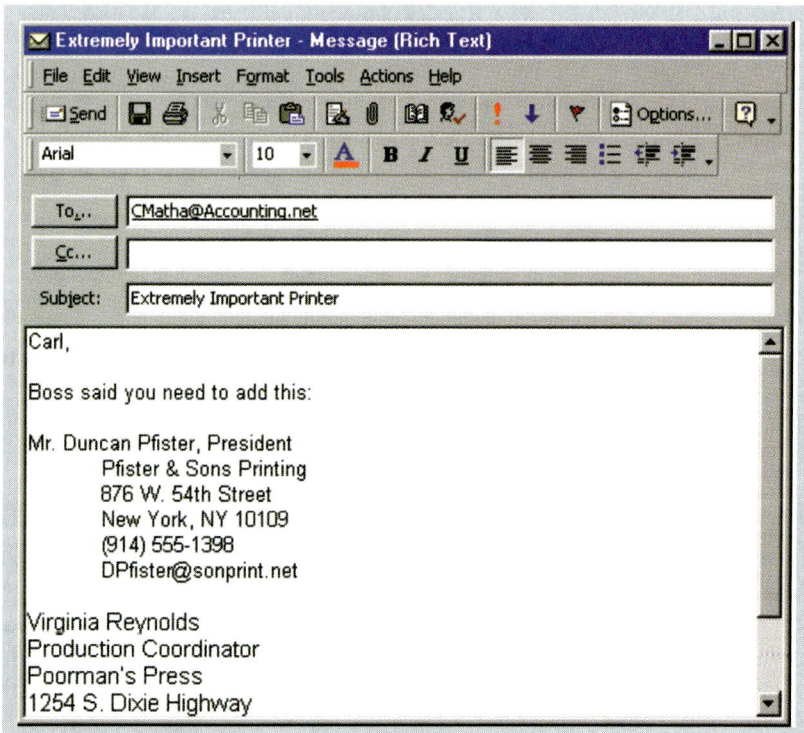

Skill Integrating Outlook Components (continued)

Do It!

14 Click [Add], then click [OK].

15 The category you need is now in the **Categories** box. Click its **check box** to add the category to Mr. Pfister's Contact form. Click [OK] to close the dialog box.

16 Click [Save and Close] when finished.

17 For the last task, click **File**, highlight **New**, and then click **Office Document**.

18 From the **New Office Document** dialog box (**Figure 4-28**), click once on **Microsoft Excel Worksheet** and then click [OK]. Click [OK] to post the document in this folder. A blank, **Excel** worksheet will open.

19 Click **cell A1** in the upper left-corner. Type: **Proposed Front List - Spring, 2004.**

20 Click **cell A3**. Type: **Book**. Press the **[Tab]** key once.

21 Type: **Author**. Press the **[Tab]** key once.

22 Type: **Proposed Publication Date**. Your worksheet should now look like **Figure 4-29**. Click the [Post] button. The **Untitled.xls** worksheet is now saved in your Inbox.

More

You could have used the **Forward** function to send JBauler's e-mail to CMatha. However, since only a small part of the e-mail was pertinent, the **Cut and Paste function** was a more appropriate choice.

The Cut and Paste function is used in conjunction with the **Office Clipboard**. The clipboard is capable of holding up to 12 items. These items are then held available for pasting. To see the clipboard, open the **View** menu, highlight **Toolbars**, and click **Clipboard**.

You can create three other Office Documents within Outlook: a **Microsoft Excel Chart**, a **Microsoft Word Document**, and a **Microsoft PowerPoint Presentation**. Before using these however, we suggest you familiarize yourself with our instructional manuals about these programs.

You can also create an **Office** document from a template. There are templates for many common documents such as letters and faxes, memos, reports, resumes, and presentations. Click **Other Shortcuts** on the **Outlook Bar** and select the **My Documents** folder. On the **Standard** toolbar, click the **down arrow** button on the **New** button. Select the **Office Document** command. In the **New Office Document** dialog box, select the tab for the type of document you want to create. Select a template. Save your document when you are finished. To return to Outlook, open the **File** menu and select the **Exit** command to close the document and exit the program. If you want to store the new document in an Outlook folder, switch to that folder before you start.

Figure 4-27 Master Category List dialog box

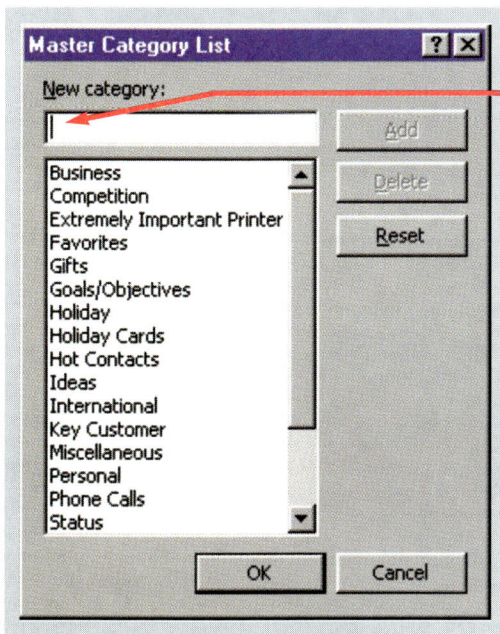

Type new category name here

Figure 4-29 Completed Excel worksheet

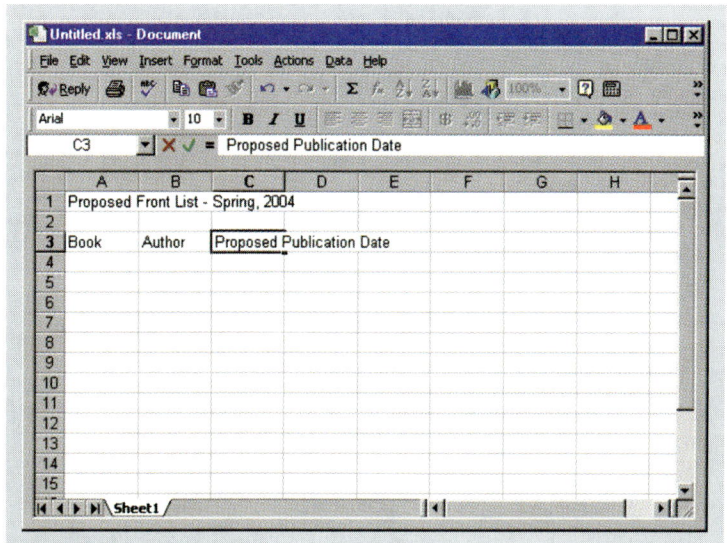

Figure 4-28 New Office Document dialog box

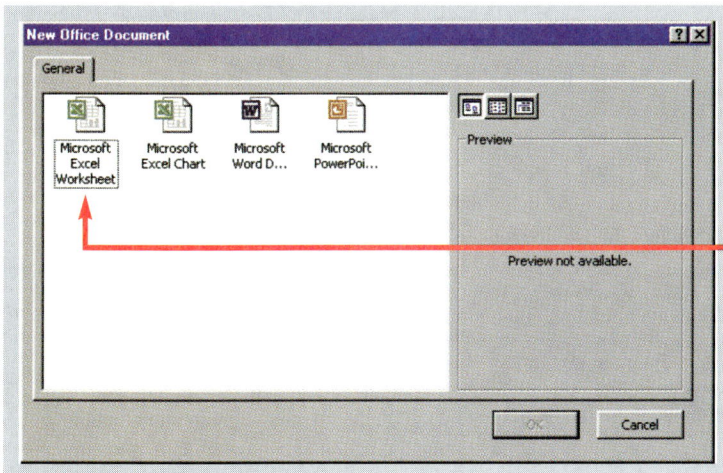

Click here if not already selected

Practice

Open the student practice file, **Prac 4-5** and follow the directions.

Hot Tip

[**Ctrl**]+[**C**] is the keyboard shortcut for the Copy command, while [**Ctrl**]+[**P**] is the keyboard shortcut for the Paste command.

Shortcuts

Function	Button/Mouse	Menu	Keyboard
Shorcut to Contacts		Click File, highlight Go To, then click Contacts	
Open new Contact form	New	Click File, highlight New, then click Contact	[Ctrl]+[N]
Shortcut to Tasks		Click View, highlight Go To, then click Task	
Open new Task form	New	Click File, highlight New, then click Task	[Ctrl]+[N]
Accept the task	✓ Accept	Click Actions, then click Accept	
Decline the task	✗ Decline	Click Actions, then click Decline	
Open a new Task Request form		Click File, highlight New, then click Task Request	[Ctrl]+[Shift]+[U]
Shortcut to Notes		Click View, highlight Go To, then click Notes	
Open a new Note	New	Click File, highlight New, then click Note	[Ctrl]+[N]

Quiz

Identify Key Features

Name the items identified by callouts in Figure 4-30

Figure 4-30 Contact form, Task form, and Note

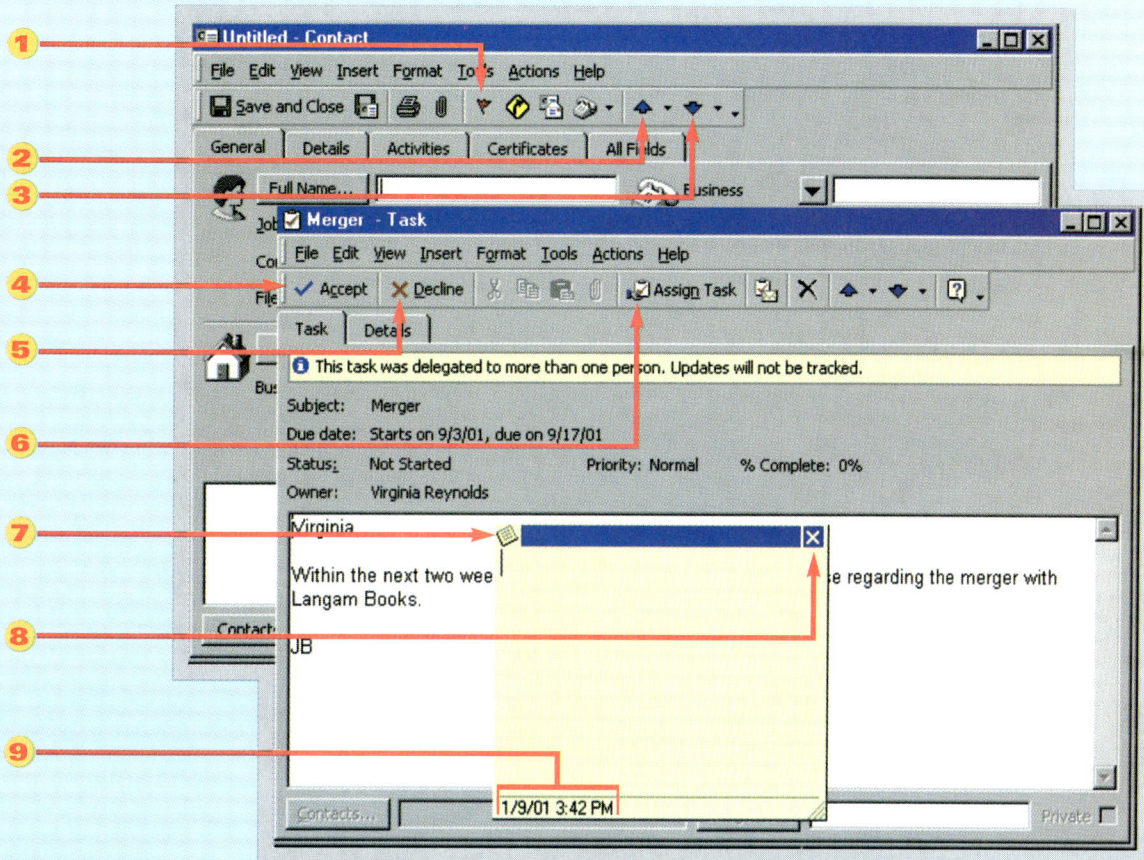

Select The Best Answer

10. Click this button if you have more than one contact to add

11. This tab on the Contact form allows you to add more information about a contact

12. This tab lists all occurrences of the contact's name in Outlook

13. An electronic business card

14. Any task that occurs at regular intervals is said to have

15. The Outlook feature that allows you to assign a job to another individual

16. Click this button to place a Task request onto your Task list

17. The default view for Contacts

a. Address Cards

b. Details

c. Accept

d. Save and New

e. Task Request form

f. Activities

g. Recurrence

h. Vcard

Quiz (continued)

Complete the Statement

18. Use this tab to encrypt e-mail and attachments you send by e-mail:
    a. Details tab
    b. Activities tab
    c. Personal tab
    d. Certificates tab

19. If you wish to see the contacts you send holiday cards to, the correct view is:
    a. Phone List view
    b. By Category view
    c. Address Cards view
    d. Follow Up Flag view

20. The correct command to insert a Vcard into outgoing mail is:
    a. Insert item
    b. Attach Vcard
    c. Insert card
    d. Edit e-mail

21. [Ctrl]+[N] will open all of the following, except:
    a. New Task form
    b. New Contact form
    c. New Note
    d. New Task Request form

22. To add the hobbies of a contact to the Contact form, click this tab first:
    a. Activities
    b. Details
    c. All Fields
    d. General

23. [Ctrl]+[Shift]+[U] is the keyboard shortcut for:
    a. New Contact form
    b. New Task form
    c. New Note form
    d. New Task Request form

24. The default order for tasks on the TaskPad is:
    a. Alphabetical
    b. Importance
    c. Date Completed
    d. Date Assigned

25. To resize a note, click and drag the:
    a. Upper-left corner of the note
    b. Upper-right corner of the note
    c. Lower-right corner of the note
    d. Lower-left corner of the note

26. All of the following are ways to view Notes, except:
    a. Subject
    b. Last Seven Days
    c. By Color
    d. By Category

27. The correct keyboard shortcut to open a new Contact form from the Inbox is:
    a. [Ctrl]+[Shift]+[I]
    b. [Ctrl]+[Shift]+[C]
    c. [Ctrl]+[Shift]+[K]
    d. [Ctrl]+[Shift]+[Y]

Interactivity

Test Your Skills

1. Add a new contact:
   a. Open the Contacts folder.
   b. Open a new, blank Contact form.
   c. Add the following: **William James, 224 Alcoa Ave., Derby, PA 24322, WJams@spud.org**.
   d. Save and close the Contact form.

2. Create a recurring task:
   a. Open the Tasks folder.
   b. Open a new, blank Task form.
   c. Add the following: **Check on illustrations for JBauler**.
   d. Set the recurrence pattern for every Tuesday and ensure that a new task is regenerated.
   e. Save and close the task.

3. Assign a task:
   a. Open the Tasks folder.
   b. Open a new, blank Task Request form.
   c. Make the due date two weeks from today.
   d. Type: **Sam, Can you check on the cost of printing a 123 page book? Ginny**.
   e. Title it: **A Job For You**.
   f. Sam's address is **SWinn@tuna.net**.
   g. Send the Task Request.

4. Create and edit a note:
   a. Open the Notes folder.
   b. Create a new note.
   c. Type: **Remind Dylan about Zimmerman on Tuesday at 8**.
   d. Change the color of the note to green.
   e. Close the note.

Interactivity (continued)

Problem Solving

1. You are the Product Liason Coordinator for Advanced Chemicals. You have been given the task of organizing the ten most important clients of the company into two categories: Supplier or Key Customer. Create ten new contacts and assign them to the appropriate categories (five in each). Provide the following information for each of the contacts: name, address, e-mail address, work phone, and spouse's name. Once you have created these contacts, view them by category.

2. You are the Project Manager for Advanced Chemicals. You have been assigned a project to demonstrate the feasibility of cold fusion energy. Divide this one task into four task requests: Preliminary Research, Product Development, Patent Search, and Potential Business. Create and assign these tasks to four different individuals on your contact list. Allow them one week only to complete their work.

3. As Product Liason Coordinator for Advanced Chemicals, you have been assigned a research project on the cost, number of employees, potential benefits, and potential drawbacks to conducting a survey of all individuals who do business with Advanced Chemicals. Divide your task into four parts and issue a task request for each part of the project to someone on your contact list. Allow them one week only to complete their work.

4. As Project Manager for Advanced Chemicals, you need to organize your contacts into two categories: Business or Hot Contact. Create ten new contacts and assign them to the appropriate categories (five in each). Provide the following information for each of the contacts: name, address, e-mail address, work phone, and spouse's name. Once you have created these contacts, view them by category.

Glossary

A

Add to Outlook Bar
A dialog box which allows you to add a shortcut to the Outlook Bar.

Address Book
A system for storing contact information in alphabetical order. There are three different address books available in Outlook, depending on the configuration of the program. The Global Address book is available in the Workgroup configuration. The Outlook Address Book is available in the Workgroup. In either the Workgroup, or the Internet Only configuration, the Outlook Address Book stores your contact information. The Personal Address Book is available in the Internet Only configuration.

Address Cards
A method of viewing contacts wherein contacts are sorted in alphabetical order and only pertinent information is shown.

Advanced Find
A dialog box which allows you to search for items in Outlook by defining advanced criteria such as, file size, or date sent.

Appointment
An activity that does not involve inviting other people or scheduling resources. Appointments may be one time or recurring.

Appointment form
An electronic form used to schedule appointments or meetings. Information entered may include: Title of meeting or appointment, duration, date, recurrence, and/or attendees invited.

Archiving
Saving information that may be needed at a later date but which will not be used often.

Attachment
Any file that is that is sent with an e-mail.

Attachments must be opened separately from e-mails.

AutoArchive
A system for automatically saving old Outlook information. Normally, it saves information that is needed later but will not be used often.

AutoPreview
Feature that allows you to see the first few lines of an unread e-mail.

B

Bcc (Blind courtesy copy)
Function that sends copies of an e-mail to multiple addresses but does not allow the recipients to view the other recipients' addresses.

C

Calendar
The section of Outlook that displays Appointments, the Date Navigator, and the TaskPad. Used for scheduling purposes.

Categories
Common characteristics that you assign to a contact for organizational purposes.

Cc (Courtesy copy)
Function that allows you to send one e-mail to multiple recipients.

Check box
A small square box that allows you to turn a dialog box option on or off by clicking it.

Click
To depress the button on your mouse while the mouse pointer is located over a desired item on the screen. Depending on the function, you may click and hold the button, click it and release it, or click and release it twice ("double-clicking").

Clipboard
A temporary storage area for cut or copied text or graphics. You can paste the contents of the Clipboard into any form in Outlook. The Windows Clipboard holds a piece of information until it is replaced by another piece of data, or until the computer is shut down. The Office Clipboard holds up to twelve pieces of data and can be viewed as a toolbar. The clipboard is common to all Microsoft Office applications.

Close
To quit an application and remove its window from the screen. You can also close a file while leaving the application open. The Close button appears in the upper-right corner of the application or form.

Contact
Any individual with whom you exchange information in either a business or personal setting.

Contact form
A form that allows you to store a variety of information about a contact.

Contacts
The section of Outlook that stores the names, addresses, and phone numbers of people in your business or personal life.

Contents tab
A Help tab that organizes Outlook's Help files by topics and subtopics, much like the table of contents in a book or outline.

Copy
To place a duplicate of a file, or portion thereof, on the Clipboard to be pasted in another location.

Create New Folder
A dialog box which allows you to create new folders in which to store information.

Cut
To remove a file, or a portion of a file, and place it on the Clipboard.

D

Date Navigator
A small monthly calendar in the Calendar Information viewer that allows you to go directly to a specific date instead of scrolling.

Deleted Items folder
The folder which temporarily stores the items you delete until you permanently delete them.

Detailed Address Cards
A method of viewing contacts in alphabetical order with more information than is available in normal Address Cards view.

Draft folder
The folder which stores e-mail messages that you have created, but not sent.

Dialog box
A box that offers additional command options for you to review or change before executing the command.

E

Ellipsis
Three dots (...) after a command that indicate a dialog box will follow with options for executing the command.

E-mail
Electronic mail. Messages sent from one computer user to another via the Internet.

Event
Any activity which lasts 24 hours or longer. Examples of events are: conventions, anniversaries, and holidays.

F

Find
A help feature in Outlook that allows you to enter words or phrases which the program will then find.

Find a Contact
An area on the Standard toolbar of the Contacts section of Outlook that allows you to find a contact by entering the first few letters of the contact's last name.

File string

A list of commands, generally preceded by a drive letter, a colon, and a backslash, telling the computer where to store, or look for, information. For example: C:\My Documents.

Flags

Icons used to identify important e-mail, contacts, etc.

Folders

Subdivisions of a disk that function as a filing system to help you organize files.

Font

A name given to a collection of text characters of a certain size, weight and style. Font has become synonymous with typeface. Arial and Times New Roman are examples of font names.

Format

The way information appears on a page. To format means to change the appearance of data without changing its content.

Forward

The act of sending an exact copy of an e-mail you received on to another individual or group

G

Global Address Book

The address book that is used in the Workgroup configuration of Outlook. The Global Address Book stores information on those people in your workgroup.

Go To Date box

A function that allows you to view any date immediately by entering it into a text box. You may enter dates in the Go To Date box in either standard date form (1/13/2005) or in the form of phrases (in three weeks).

H

Highlight

To select a segment of text for a particular use by dragging your mouse over it with the button depressed.

HTML (HyperText Markup Language)

The source code, or programming language, used to create and reproduce Web pages. A browser, such as Internet Explorer, interprets HTML to create the displays you see.

I

Icon

An object on the Windows desktop that represents a file, folder or application. Also, a loosely used term for some objects displayed in Web pages.

Inbox

The section of Outlook that stores your e-mail.

Index

A Help tab that lists all of Outlook's Help topics alphabetically.

Insertion point

A vertical blinking line on the screen that indicates where text and graphics will be inserted. The insertion point also indicates where an action will begin.

Internet

An extended world-wide computer network that is composed of numerous smaller networks. The World Wide Web is part of the Internet.

Internet connection

The means by which your computer (the client) is connected to a Web or e-mail server, either through a network or by the use of a modem.

ISP (Internet Service Provider)

A company, school or other entity that provides access to an Internet server, often for a fee.

J

Journal

The section of Outlook that displays a history of your recorded activities. Activities are displayed in a timeline format.

K

Keyboard shortcuts
A feature that allows you to access different areas of Outlook by pressing one, two, or three keys at once. For example, holding down the Control key while simultaneously depressing the N key will open a new, blank e-mail form in the Inbox section. However, [Ctrl]+[N] will open a new, blank contact form if you are in the Contacts portion of Outlook, while [Ctrl]+[N] will open a new Appointment form in the Calendar section.

L

Launch
To start a program so you can work with it.

M

Master Categories List
A list of categories that you can assign to contacts in Outlook to make organizing contacts easier. You can also edit this list to add or delete categories.

Maximize
To display a window across your entire screen.

Meeting
Any activity in which you invite others or for which you reserve resources. Meetings may be face-to-face or online.

Menu
A list of related application commands.

Menu bar
Lists the names of menus containing application commands. Click a Menu name on the Menu bar to display its list of commands.

Message form
The template upon which e-mail messages are created

Microsoft Outlook
An application from Microsoft that handles e-mail, tasks, and scheduling, among other functions.

Minimize
To remove a window (containing an active file, folder or application) from the desktop without closing or exiting it. A minimized window is represented as a button on the status bar at the bottom of the Windows display.

Mouse
A pointing device that converts the movement of your hand into movements of a pointer or cursor on the screen, and includes one or more buttons used to actuate graphical controls.

Mouse pointer
The cursor on your screen, usually arrow shaped, that you control by guiding the mouse on your desk. You use the mouse pointer to select items, drag objects, choose commands, and start or exit programs. The shape of the mouse pointer can change depending on the task being executed.

My Computer shortcuts
The area on the Outlook Bar that provides access to the file, folders and drives on your computer.

My Documents shortcut
The area on the Outlook Bar that provides access to the My Documents folder on your hard drive.

My Shortcuts group
The area on the Outlook Bar that provides shortcuts to Drafts, Journal, Sent Items, and the Outbox.

N

Network
A group of computers linked together to share data.

New Office Document
A dialog box that allows you to access and post a new office application. Using this dialog box, you can access an Excel worksheet, a Word document, or a PowerPoint presentation.

Note
A short, concise piece of information stored electronically in the form of a sticky note.

Notes
The section of Outlook where electronic sticky notes are stored.

O

Office Assistant

An animated representation of the Microsoft Office 2000 Help facility. The Office Assistant provides hints, instructions, and a convenient interface between the user and Outlook's various help facilities.

Open

Command used to access a file that has already been created and saved on disk.

Other Shortcuts group

The area on the Outlook bar that provides shortcuts to My Computer, My Documents, and Favorites.

Outbox

The section of Outlook that stores e-mail until you are connected to your mail server.

Outlook Bar

The section of Outlook to the left of the Information viewer that stores shortcuts

Outlook Shortcuts group

The area on the Outlook Bar that provides shortcuts to Notes, Tasks, Deleted Items, Calendar, Contacts, Inbox and Outlook Today.

Outlook Today

The section of Outlook that provides an overview of your e-mail messages, tasks, and the Calendar. By default, shows the current day's activities.

P

Page Setup

A dialog box used with the Print function to designate the desired characteristics (page orientation, color selection, etc.) of the page or pages you are printing.

Paste

To insert cut or copied data into other locations.

Personal Address Book

The address book that Outlook uses when configured for Internet Only E-mail Service.

Plan a Meeting

A dialog box that allows you to schedule a meeting and notify (by email) those required to attend. You can access this function from the Calendar section by opening the Action menu and clicking on Plan a Meeting.

Pop-up menu

A group of command options that appears, if available, when the user clicks the right mouse button. This menu usually pertains directly to the object that was clicked.

Preview pane

The function that allows you to see the entire text of an e-mail without actually opening it.

Print

To send a file, picture or other data to a properly connected printer device so that it will be reproduced on paper.

Print Preview

Allows you to view material as it will appear when printed on a sheet of paper.

Printer

A peripheral device that reproduces data from the computer onto paper.

Program

A software application that performs specific tasks, such as Microsoft Word or Microsoft Outlook.

Programs menu

A menu on the Windows 95 or Windows 98 Start menu that lists the applications on your computer such as Microsoft Outlook.

R

Radio button

A small circular button in a dialog box that allows you to turn options on or off.

RAM (random access memory)

The memory that programs use to function while the computer is on. When you shut down the computer, all information in RAM is lost.

Recall This Message

A feature of Outlook which allows you to recall an e-mail which has not yet been read by the recipient.

Recurrence

The state in which an appointment or task occurs more than once on a regular basis. For example, an appointment that occurs every Monday at 8 AM is said to have recurrence.

Reminder Notice

The dialog box which reminds you of important meetings, events, or appointments prior to their occurence. Once on the screen, you have the option to open the appointment, dismiss the reminder, or "snooze" and have the reminder appear again in five minutes.

Reminders

The function that allows you to be forewarned of impending appointments, meetings, events, or tasks. Reminders can be set anywhere from five minutes to two days before the activity begins.

Right-click

To click the right mouse button; often used to access specialized menus and shortcuts.

Run

To start an application.

S

Save

Stores changes you have made to a file maintaining the file's current name and location.

Save As

Command used to save a new file for the first time or to create a duplicate copy of a file that has already been saved.

Save as Web Page

The File menu command which automatically converts your calendar, or Task list into HTML for publication on the World Wide Web.

A graphical device for moving vertically and horizontally through a document with the mouse. Scroll bars are located along the right and bottom edges of the document window.

Select a Stationery

A dialog box that allows you to choose electronic stationery of varying designs upon which to create e-mail

Select Attendees and Resources

A dialog box that works in conjunction with the Plan a Meeting dialog box and allows you to indicate whether or not an individual is required to attend a specific meeting or event. This dialog box also allows you to "invite" resources, such as meeting rooms, or overhead projectors.

Sent Items folder

The section of Outlook that stores copies of e-mail that has been sent.

Signature

A section of e-mail that you create which contains your name and contact information. By creating and using a signature you eliminate the need to retype your contact information on every e-mail.

Start

To open an application for use.

Start button

A button on the taskbar that accesses a special menu that you use to start programs, find files, access Windows Help and more.

Submenu

A menu that appears when a menu item is highlighted; for example, on the Start Menu, you can highlight "Programs" to bring up a submenu of available applications.

T

Task

An activity or job that you must complete in your work or personal life which has a definite time frame for completion.

Scroll bar

Task Recurrence

A dialog box which allows you to set the recurrence of tasks. You can also regenerate a new task to replace the recurring task that is completed.

Task Request form

A special e-mail form that allows you to assign a task to another individual or group.

Taskbar

A bar, usually located at the bottom of the screen, that contains the Start button. It shows which programs are running by displaying their program buttons, and shows the current time.

TaskPad

An area in the Calendar section of Outlook which stores the daily or recurring tasks that are entered.

Tasks

The section of Outlook that stores a list of activities that you must complete, or activities you have assigned to others.

Text box

A rectangular area in which text is added so that it may be manipulated independently of the rest of a document.

Title bar

The horizontal bar at the top of a window that displays the name of the document or application that appears in the window.

Toolbar

A graphical bar containing buttons that act as shortcuts for common commands.

V

Vcard

A completed Contact form sent to another individual. Sometimes called an electronic business card.

W

Window

The graphical representation of a particular file, folder or application when it is active on the Windows desktop.

Windows

A popular operating system for PC-based computers, produced by Microsoft. Different versions of Windows include Windows 3.1, Windows 95 and Windows 98.

World Wide Web (WWW, or the Web)

An enormous array of linked hypertext documents that reside on computers around the world, all of which can be viewed using a browser application such as Internet Explorer.

Index

Notes • Notes